Who?
What?
Where?
Bible
Quizzes

Who? What? Where? Bible Quizzes

MAX STILSON

BAKER BOOK HOUSE
Grand Rapids, Michigan 49506

Copyright 1960 by
Baker Book House Company

Mass market edition:
Second printing, October 1982

ISBN: 0-8010-8012-6

PHOTOLITHOPRINTED BY CUSHING - MALLOY, INC.
ANN ARBOR, MICHIGAN, UNITED STATES OF AMERICA

INTRODUCTION

How many times have you thought of a Bible reference or story and couldn't recall who?

These quizzes will help you to remember the who's of the Bible.

These quizzes can be used for your Sunday School Class, Young People's Society or you can study them over individually to increase your own Bible knowledge.

The purpose of these quizzes is to help you to know the word of God better. You will remember these quizzes longer than any other method of study. Look up the references and read the stories or events that these quizzes are taken from.

Score five (5) points for each question that you can answer successfully. If you don't know the answer, don't skip over them, but learn the answer. You will be a stronger and better equipped Christian for having taken the time to master the word of God.

M. S.

WHO? WHAT? WHERE? BIBLE QUIZ

Quiz #1

1. Who bore witness to the light?
2. Who was the brother of John?
3. Who was the first martyred of the Apostles?
4. Who was Timothy's grandmother?
5. Who killed Abel?
6. Who had a coat of many colors?
7. Who fell off a seat backwards and broke his neck?
8. Who was the queen of the Ethiopians under whom Philip served?
9. Who called himself a "prisoner of the Lord Jesus Christ"?
10. Who was smitten with leprosy because she spoke against Moses?
11. Who is called "the beloved physician"?
12. Who was a seller of purple of Thyatira?
13. Who was killed by King Herod with a sword?
14. Who was sent from God to tell Mary of the birth of Jesus?
15. Who asked her daughter to ask king Herod for the head of John the Baptist on a charger?
16. Who went with Barnabas into Cyprus after Paul and Barnabas separated?
17. Who became lame when his nurse dropped him?
18. Who was the oldest man who ever lived?
19. Who let David down through a window so that he escaped King Saul who was trying to kill him?
20. Who raised Esther after her parents died?

Quiz #2

1. Who lifted the serpent in the wilderness?
2. Who took the gifts to the sufferers in Jerusalem?
3. Who was David's great grandmother?
4. Who walked on the water to go to Jesus but became afraid and cried for Jesus to save him?

7

WHO? WHAT? WHERE? BIBLE QUIZ

5. Who did Paul almost persuade to become a Christian?
6. Who was the queen who made a feast for the women in the royal house which belonged to King Ahasuerus?
7. Who did Jael kill with a nail and hammer?
8. Who did the Lord first raise up as Israel's deliverer?
9. Who in scripture is compared to fruit trees?
10. Who was the armour-bearer of Saul?
11. Who inherited the great riches of Abraham?
12. Who was waiting on the side of the mountain when Moses came down?
13. Who did David purchase a threshing floor from on which he erected an altar?
14. Who was the prophet of Israel who induced the army of Israel to treat their captives from Judah kindly and return them to their countrymen?
15. Who does Isaiah refer to as the Holy One of Israel?
16. Who was the king of Israel, when the word of the Lord came to Hosea?
17. Who did the angel of the Lord smite and was eaten by worms and gave up the ghost?
18. Who saved two hundred seventy-six (276) people from shipwreck by his faith and wise counsel?
19. Who dreamed of a ladder reaching to heaven?
20. Who did Jesus call "a fox"?

Quiz #3

1. Who thought that he heard Eli the priest calling him when it was really God?
2. Who led an army that was armed with lamps and pitchers?
3. Who was described as "Behold an Israelite, indeed, in which is no guile"?
4. Who was Ruth's second husband?

8

5. Who went to Pilate, begged the body of Jesus and wrapped it in a clean linen cloth?
6. Who was Israel's second judge?
7. Who slew Absalom?
8. Who was the representative prince of the tribe of Benjamin in the wilderness?
9. Who was the inventor of Nomadic music?
10. Who was king of Judah when the word of the Lord came to Zephaniah?
11. Who sold Joseph into Egypt?
12. Who told king Lemuel not to drink wine?
13. Who said in his heart, "There is no God"?
14. Who was sold into the hand of a woman?
15. Who spoke against the Apostle John with malicious words?
16. Who had a vision of a flying roll?
17. Who told Israel that their old men would dream dreams and their young men would see visions?
18. Who did Paul circumcise?
19. Who did Paul keep from committing suicide?
20. Who suffered many things in a dream because of Jesus?

Quiz #4

1. Who baptized Jesus?
2. Who is known as the "Beloved Apostle"?
3. Who is known for the great test he made between the true religion of Jehovah and the false religion of Baal?
4. Who annointed Samuel as king?
5. Who was the goddess that the Ephesians worshipped?
6. Who led the Israelites into the promised land?
7. Who was a godly Roman centurion of Caesarea?
8. Who changed water into wine?
9. Who was Israel's third judge?

9

10. Who had thirty sons who rode on thirty ass colts?
11. Who climbed up in a Sycamore tree to see Jesus?
12. Who did Reuben, Jacob's eldest son, commit the act of adultery with?
13. Who was king of Judah when Amos prophesied?
14. Who made a navy of ships on the shore of the Red Sea?
15. Who heard God's voice in the cool of the day?
16. Who was the first of all the prophets?
17. Who prophesied before the captivity?
18. Who prophesied during the captivity?
19. Who prophesied after the captivity?
20. Who was the master of the eunuchs of king Nebuchadnezzar?

Quiz #5

1. Who became the leader of the children of Israel after Moses died?
2. Who was David's very close friend?
3. Who was the silversmith of Ephesus who became wealthy by making silver shrines of the goddess, Diana?
4. Who was the only woman judge of the children of Israel?
5. Who destroyed all her grandchildren except Joash?
6. Who expected Paul to give him a sum of money?
7. Who slew the brother of Goliath?
8. Who were called "the sons of thunder"?
9. Who told the children of Israel that the land of Canaan flowed with milk and honey?
10. Who was the fourth judge of Israel?
11. Who owned the tomb in which Jesus was buried?
12. Who built the town of Beth-horon?
13. Who was the chief of Pharaoh's bodyguard, who bought Joseph from Midianites and placed him in charge of the household.
14. Who cursed the serpent in the Garden of Eden?

WHO? WHAT? WHERE? BIBLE QUIZ

15. Who built Nineveh?
16. Who referred to himself as the Morasthite?
17. Who was smitten with leprosy for unlawfully invading the holy precincts of the Temple?
18. Who was known as "pillars of the early church"?
19. Who was Moses angry with because they did eat the sin offering in the Holy Place?
20. Who did God tell that man looketh on the outward appearance, but God looketh on the heart?

Quiz #6

1. Who was cast into the lion's den?
2. Who was the ruler of Egypt when Moses brought the children of Israel out of Egypt?
3. Who reported, "There is a lad here with food"?
4. Who under the wicked influence of his wife made the worship of Baal the state religion?
5. Who interpreted the dream of King Nebuchadnezzar and was made ruler over Babylon?
6. Who slew the giant Goliath with a sling and a stone?
7. Who was taken up by a whirlwind into heaven?
8. Who multiplied the widow's oil so that she could sell it to pay her debts?
9. Who did Peter raise from the dead?
10. Who did Deborah call to be the fifth judge of Israel?
11. Who was the prophet who rent his own garment in twelve pieces and directed Jeroboam to take ten as an indication that he should be king over ten tribes?
12. Who was referred to as a migthy hunter before the Lord?
13. Who was known as the Elkashite?
14. Who was imprisoned twice by the Jewish council?

11

15. Who visited the schools of the prophets of Gilgal, Bethel and Jericho?
16. Who told the Jews to judge Jesus according to their law?
17. Who was in prison with Paul when they were released by a great earthquake which opened the prison doors?
18. Who was absent when Jesus appeared to His disciples after his resurrection?
19. Who did Paul leave in Crete to set things in order?
20. Who drove the giants out of Hebron?

Quiz #7

1. Who was the Roman ruler before whom Jesus was tried?
2. Who was the man who built an ark before the flood?
3. Who did Jesus see sitting under a fig tree before he knew him?
4. Who is the father of lying?
5. Who used a chest to collect money for the repair of the temple and the restoration of the worship of the true God?
6. Who fled into Egypt to escape Solomon who was trying to kill him?
7. Who was the teacher of Paul?
8. Who had his life saved three times by his donkey?
9. Who was the sixth judge of Israel?
10. Who protected Jeremiah when the priests and false prophets demanded Jeremiah's death?
11. Who did Jehoiakim send into Egypt to bring back Urijah who Jehoiakim slew with a sword?
12. Who drove the cart on which David was taking the ark to Jerusalem?
13. Who asked if any good thing could come out of Nazareth?
14. Who turned Solomon's heart after other gods?
15. Who has been called "the disobedient prophet"?

12

16. Who did Jezebel proclaim a fast for and had two men stoned so that Ahab could take possession of his vineyard?
17. Who brought a mixture of myrrh and aloes to be used in Christ's burial?
18. Who is the angel of the bottomless pit in the Hebrew tongue?
19. Who was the captain of the host of the king of Syria?
20. Who was cast into prison for sedition made in the city and for murder?

Quiz #8

1. Who betrayed Jesus?
2. Who was the man who was willing to sacrifice his own son?
3. Who was converted while on his way to Damascus?
4. Who fell asleep during a sermon and fell out of a window?
5. Who hid Joash and his nurse so that Athaliah could not slay him?
6. Who sold his land and brought his money and laid it at the feet of the Apostles?
7. Who was the blind beggar of Jericho who was healed by Jesus?
8. Who was the seventh judge of Israel?
9. Who was Rebekah's nurse?
10. Who is the angel of the bottomless pit in the Greek language?
11. Who had four unmarried daughters who were prophetesses?
12. Who offered the aged Jacob a guarantee for the safety of Benjamin?
13. Who was the Ethiopian eunuch who drew the prophet Jeremiah out of a dungeon by cords?
14. Who challenged the prophets of Baal in a contest to see if God would answer them by fire?
15. Who was punished because he did not restrain his vile sons?
16. Who were the first apostles arrested and imprisoned?
17. Who was able to heal the sick by casting his shadow over them?

WHO? WHAT? WHERE? BIBLE QUIZ

18. Who did the Lord give a choice of three evils on account of his sin against him?
19. Who did Samuel hew in pieces before the Lord in Gilgal?
20. Who were the two prophets who encouraged Zerubbabel to complete rebuilding the temple?

Quiz #9

1. Who was the prophet who rebuked David for his sins?
2. Who made havoc of the early church?
3. Who anointed Jesus with ointment, and wiped His feet with her hair?
4. Who was the high priest at the time of Christ's death?
5. Who erected a golden calf at Bethel and at Dan?
6. Who was responsible for the division of the kingdom of Israel?
7. Who was the only woman not born of woman?
8. Who was called a "madman" by a Roman ruler?
9. Who did Paul call a "child of the devil"?
10. Who is the king who made a great feast to a thousand of his lords?
11. Who brought an offering of the fruit of the ground which God rejected?
12. Who was the eigth judge of Israel?
13. Who was the first high priest?
14. Who was chosen as the minstrel of Saul?
15. Who was the handmaid who Leah gave to Jacob as wife and she bore him two sons — Gad and Asher?
16. Who was Paul's secretary who penned the Epistle to the Roman's and inserted a personal greeting in it?
17. Who was cast into a great pit which was covered with stones when he died?
18. Who told Job to curse God and die?

19. Who lost two sons because they offered strange fires before the Lord?
20. Who commanded the children of Israel to eat unleavened bread at the passover feast?

Quiz #10

1. Who made a vow that resulted in him killing his own daughter?
2. Who was the wife of Uriah the Hittite?
3. Who was chosen to take the place of Judas Iscariot?
4. Who sought to wrest the throne from King David?
5. Who was Paul's son in the faith?
6. Who was compelled to bear Christ's cross?
7. Who refused to give bread and water to David's men?
8. Who was Abraham's rightful heir, and child of promise?
9. Who met Moses on his return to Egypt?
10. Who came to Zacharias to announce the birth of John the Baptist?
11. Who did David send to beseige Rabbah?
12. Who was the god of Ekron?
13. Who was the palace functionary who had charge of Herod Agrippa's bedchamber?
14. Who danced before Herod and was granted her request for the head of John the Baptist?
15. Who received the body of Saul and his three sons from the Philistines?
16. Who first discovered the empty tomb of Jesus after His resurrection?
17. Who made the coats of skins for Adam and Eve?
18. Who discovered the lost book of the law which led to a reformation and the temporary abolition of idolatry?
19. Who was king of Judah when Nebuchadnezzar beseiged Jerusalem?

20. Who brought Nehemiah messages of the Jews which were left of the captivity?

Quiz #11

1. Who went out from the trial of Jesus and wept bitterly?
2. Who came preaching in the wilderness, clothed in camel's hair?
3. Who assisted Moses in his work?
4. Who wrestled all night without knowing with whom he was wrestling?
5. Who dwelt in the plain of Jordan and pitched his tent toward Sodom?
6. Who caused iron to swim?
7. Who rebuilt king Solomon's temple?
8. Who was the God of Israel after Gideon died?
9. Who today are the descendants of Ishmael?
10. Who was the champion of the army of the Philistines?
11. Who built the first city?
12. Who slew Zachariah, the last of Jehu's dynasty?
13. Who was the last king of Israel?
14. Who built Schechem in mount Ephraim?
15. Who was taken captive by the Amalekites at Ziklag and was later rescued by her husband after he had defeated the enemy?
16. Who was the king of Gerar at whose court Abraham attempted to pass Sarah off as his sister?
17. Who was the wife of Jehoram, daughter of Ahab and granddaughter of Omri?
18. Who did the prince of the Babylonian eunuchs give the name of Belteshazzar to?
19. Who was the father of the Ammonite tribe?
20. Who did Bilhah commit sin with?

Quiz #12

1. Who ate locust and wild honey?
2. Who was released from prison in place of Jesus?
3. Who was the ninth judge of Israel?
4. Who was employed to attend upon King David when he was old and declining in vitality?
5. Who was the deity of Moab, whom the children of Israel became attracted to at Shittum, which caused the death of twenty four thousand (24,000) in a plague?
6. Who was the Moabite king who lured Balaam from Pethro to curse Israel?
7. Who did Gideon slay at a winepress?
8. Who gave Israel their first lessons in metallurgy?
9. Who was the priest-king of Salem who received tithes from Abraham returning from the battle of the kings and brought him bread and wine and gave him a blessing in the name of "the most high God".?
10. Who killed Sennecherib?
11. Who did the Jerusalem magistrates send to release Paul from jail?
12. Who was the chamberlain who was in charge of the harem of Ahasuerus in Esther's day?
13. Who commanded that the three Hebrew children were to be cast into the fiery furnace?
14. Who attempted to duplicate the gold-buying projects of Solomon but lost his fleet before he set sail?
15. Who did Caleb give to his halfbrother as a reward for winning Kiriath-sepher?
16. Who was the father of the aged Jerusalem prophetess, Anna?
17. Who did Paul heal on the island of Melita (Malta)?
18. Who is Lord of the Sabbath?
19. Who was king of Israel when Amos prophesied?

WHO? WHAT? WHERE? BIBLE QUIZ

20. Who was the keeper of the king's forest whom Nehemiah took a letter of introduction from Artaxerxes to get the timber to make the beams for the gates of the palace?

Quiz #13

1. Who was the Roman ruler when Jesus was born?
2. Who kept the money bag for the disciples?
3. Who is called the god of this world?
4. Who was the tenth judge of Israel?
5. Who was commander-in-chief of the army of Saul?
6. Who did Asa send all the silver and gold of the treasury to?
7. Who served as scribal secretary of state who was responsible for turning over to Hilkiah, the priest, the money paid by the people for repairing the temple?
8. Who trained Timothy in the faith inherited from her mother?
9. Who sent masons, carpenters, cedars, and firs from Lebanon to David for a house?
10. Who did the unbelieving Jews of Thessalonica drag out of his house because he testified of Christ?
11. Who was the father of two daughters, Zeruiah and Abigail, who became the mothers of famous warriors?
12. Who did David send to Mizpeh of Moab for protection when he was being hunted down by angry Saul?
13. Who served the order for Naboth to be stoned?
14. Who did Jesus say was his brother, sister, and mother?
15. Who was head and shoulders above all his people?
16. Who did God prepare a gourd for to hold over that it might be a shadow over his head to deliver him from his grief?
17. Who told his brothers to cast Joseph into a pit?
18. Who told Jesus that the dogs under her table ate of the children's crumbs?
19. Who waited on the wife of Naaman, the leper?

20. Who did David set in the forefront of the hottest battle, so that he would be killed?

Quiz #14

1. Who was hung on his own gallows?
2. Who had his own brother murdered?
3. Who healed a cripple and was worshipped as god?
4. Who challenged the other disciples to accompany Christ to the place of His execution?
5. Who washed his hand before the multitude and said that he was innocent of the blood of a just person?
6. Who was sold to the Ishmaelites for twenty pieces of silver?
7. Who was sick unto death and the Lord added fifteen years to his life?
8. Who was set down in the midst of a valley full of dry bones?
9. Who was cast into the dungeon of Malchiah and sunk in the mire?
10. Who received his speech after writing his son's name?
11. Who was turned into a pillar of salt?
12. Who was the brother of James, the son of Zebedee?
13. Who danced before Herod on his birthday?
14. Who was the father of King Saul?
15. Who came to Jerusalem with a great train, camels, gold and precious stones to visit Solomon?
16. Who were the two men chosen to replace Judas Iscariot?
17. Who was the eleventh judge of Israel?
18. Who committed the first murder?
19. Who proclaimed Saul's son, Ish-bosheth, king at Mahanaim?
20. Who prophesied against Memphis and its fallen images?

Quiz #15

1. Who ate the shew-bread?

2. Who were the two Egyptian magicians who attempted to counterwork Moses?
3. Who found Moses as a baby in the river?
4. Who was the mother of Moses and Aaron?
5. Who is the prince of life?
6. Who was the master of Joseph while he was a slave?
7. Who was the steward of Abram's house?
8. Who was the twelfth judge of Israel?
9. Who was the master of the eunuchs at Babylon during Nebuchadnezzar's reign?
10. Who did the mob demand Pilate to release instead of Jesus?
11. Who did Abraham make a covenant with at Beer-sheba?
12. Who was the head of the guard who escorted Solomon to Gihon to be anointed king?
13. Who was Rachel's maidservant who at her mistress's desire became one of Jacob's secondary wives and the mother of Dan and Naphtali?
14. Who did Paul leave his cloak with in Troas which he afterward sent for?
15. Who became head of a tribe and required his people to dwell in tents, refrain from agriculture and abstain from wine, in order to preserve primitive simplicity of manners?
16. Who killed a young lion with his bare hands?
17. Who was the skilled musician of Saul's court who married his daughter?
18. Who was the early teacher of Saul of Tarsus?
19. Who did Nebuchadnezzar appoint governor of Palestine after the destruction of Jerusalem in 587 B. C.?
20. Who carried a letter from Zedekiah to the exiles in Babylon?

Quiz #16

1. Who is called the "Father of many nations"?

WHO? WHAT? WHERE? BIBLE QUIZ

2. Who was the thirteenth judge of Israel?
3. Who was the high Assyrian dignitary who settled various tribes in Samaria?
4. Who was the governor of the Shechem in the time of Abimelech to whom he showed unswerving fidelity?
5. Who reserved a room for Elisha to use when he was traveling and passed by?
6. Who were the two quarreling women in the church at Phillipi?
7. Who built the judgement hall where Felix presided over the trial of Paul?
8. Who did Jesus send the twelve apostles to preach to?
9. Who was the Arabian opponent of Nehemiah's who ridiculed the plan to rebuild Jerusalem's wall and plotted against Nehemiah?
10. Who was the captain of the guard of Pharaoh?
11. Who called Paul a ringleader of the sect of the Nazarenes?
12. Who did Jesus ask to care for his mother at his Crucifixion?
13. Who did Mary visit before Jesus was born?
14. Who was called the "son of the morning"?
15. Who was the prophet of the Old Testament who foretold Christ's triumphal entry into Jerusalem?
16. Who was the woman who played an important part in the trial of Jesus?
17. Who found a piece of money in the mouth of a fish?
18. Who warned Peter and foretold his fall?
19. Who was the Old Testament prophet who saved some people from ptomaine poisoning?
20. Who was saved by a miraculous well of water in the wilderness?

Quiz #17

1. Who came to Jesus by night?
2. Who sold his birthright for a mess of pottage?

3. Who wrote letters in her husband's name and had Naboth carried out of the city and stoned to death?
4. Who tried to purchase the gift of the Holy Ghost with money?
5. Who baptized Saul?
6. Who called to Moses out of a burning bush?
7. Who was the author of the maxims contained in Proverb 30?
8. Who were the gods of Avva?
9. Who was the custodian of the olive and sycamore trees under King David?
10. Who asked Jesus if he wished them to "command fire to come down from heaven and consume" the inhospitable Samaritans of a certain village?
11. Who was the king of Zeboum who with the confederated kings of the cities of the Dead Sea plain was defeated by Chedorlaomer?
12. Who was dispatched to Jeremiah by king Zedekiah to query the prophet concerning the outcome of Nebuchadnezzar's attack on Jerusalem?
13. Who warned Paul of the plot of forty men to kill him?
14. Who was John's faithful martyr in Pergamos?
15. Who was the queen of heaven?
16. Who did David appoint over his guard?
17. Who circumsized Moses?
18. Who was both a king and a priest?
19. Who longed for a drink of water and refused it when it was brought unto him?
20. Who was the first man to have two wives?

Quiz #18

1. Who named the birds and beasts?
2. Who judged after the flesh?
3. Who made a vow that if God be with him, he would give him a tenth of what he had?

WHO? WHAT? WHERE? BIBLE QUIZ

4. Who stole her father's images and put them in the camel's furniture and sat on them so that her father couldn't find them?
5. Who drew water for all of the camels of Abraham's servant and offered him a room to lodge in?
6. Who did Miriam get to take care of Moses after Pharaoh's nurse found him the river?
7. Who fell through a lattice in his palace and was seriously injured?
8. Who was the scribe who wrote the prophecies of Jeremiah at the prophet's dictation?
9. Who was the chief of the guard who executed Adonijah, Joab and Shimer?
10. Who delivered the epistle to the Ephesians for Paul?
11. Who struck Jeremiah and put him in the stocks, but later released him?
12. Who accompanied Paul on his second missionary journey?
13. Who assassinated Pekahiah?
14. Who was governor of Syria when Jesus was born?
15. Who was compelled to carry Christ's cross to Golgotha?
16. Who was the treasurer under Cyrus, king of Persia, through whom the sacred vessels were restorted to the Jews?
17. Who was the first song-writer?
18. Who committed suicide by falling on his won sword?
19. Who was healed when a lump of figs was laid on a boil?
20. Who told Philip that they desired to see Jesus?

WHAT? BIBLE QUIZ

INTRODUCTION

What happened! What does it mean!

Have you ever thought these questions as you have read your Bible?

The questions contained in this quizbook will help to answer some of your questions.

See how many you can correctly answer. Score yourself five (5) points for each one that you can answer correctly. Do not be discouraged if you need to study the word of God.

Study the questions and answers until you can answer them correctly.

This book can be used in your Young People's groups, Sunday School class, your family devotions or for your own individual study.

Master the word of God for strength of character. There is a wonderful experience for you as you study the word of God and come to know and love Him whom the Bible points you to.

M. S.

WHO? WHAT? WHERE? BIBLE QUIZ

Quiz #1

1. What was the name of the well at which Jesus talked to the woman of Samaria?
2. What great teachings are found in the twentieth (20th) chapter of Exodus?
3. What was another name for Simon?
4. What is the Greek title for the book of Revelation?
5. What did the Apostles first do after the ascension of Jesus?
6. What two (2) treasure cities were built for Pharaoh?
7. What was a physical characteristic of Ehud, the second (2nd) judge of Israel?
8. What should the prayer of every christian be?
9. What did the men of Ephraim threaten to do to Jephthan, because he did not call them to fight against the children of Ammon?
10. What wicked act was Rachel guilty of?
11. What tribe was Moses and Aaron members of?
12. What sorrowful event happened to the wife of Phinehas?
13. What tribe was Saul a member of?
14. What effect did Saul's death have on David?
15. What sins did Malachi reprove the people of?
16. What did the Lord command the children of Israel to make that they might keep in remembrance his commandments?
17. What did the king of Jericho order Rahab to do with the two (2) spies whom she was hiding?
18. What city was unsuccessfully attacked by Joshua because of the sin of Achan?
19. What kind of wood did Solomon use to make the pillars and balustrades of the temple?
20. What river formed the border between Moab and the Amorites?

WHO? WHAT? WHERE? BIBLE QUIZ

Quiz #2

1. What did Jesus say a man must do to see the kingdom of God?
2. What was the word the Ephraimites were forced to use which betrayed their nationality?
3. What weapon did Christ use when he met Satan in His great temptation in the wilderness?
4. What was the greatest trial that Abraham's faith experienced?
5. What occupation did the children of Israel have under the Egyptians?
6. What did David do to the young man who by his own confession had killed Saul?
7. What did the Lord reprove Samuel for?
8. What sin did Dathan, Abiram and On commit?
9. What is atonement?
10. What did the children of Israel use to dig a well at Beer?
11. What is a beka?
12. What name did Rachel give to Benjamin when he was born?
13. What was the sign of the ship that Paul traveled on from Alexandria to Syracuse?
14. What church was Phebe a servant in?
15. What stone was used as the foundation of the wall of the city of the New Jerusalem?
16. What was the chief physical characteristic of Zacchaeus?
17. What did the multitudes accuse Jesus of before Pilate?
18. What did Balak offer on each of the seven (7) altars which he erected on Mt. Pisgah?
19. What were the names of the four (4) rivers which flower from the Garden of Eden?
20. What is another name for the Red Sea that Isaiah used?

Quiz #3

1. What did Jesus say men should do about the scriptures?

WHO? WHAT? WHERE? BIBLE QUIZ

2. What woman was the fourth (4th) judge of Israel?
3. What magnificient building stood on Mt. Moriah?
4. What beautiful edifice now stands on Mt. Moriah?
5. What excuse did Rebekah make to Isaac for wanting to send Jacob away?
6. What divine ordinance in the Christian church takes the place of the passover?
7. What is the meaning of the word passover?
8. What nation did the Lord send Saul to destroy?
9. What did Moses command Aaron to do when he knew that judgment was about to fall on the people?
10. What effect did the playing of the harp by David have on King Saul?
11. What promise did the two (2) spies give Rahab for hiding them from the king?
12. What did the priests purchase with the thirty (30) pieces of silver which Judas cast down in the temple?
13. What is a bath?
14. What was the punishment for blasphemy under the Mosiac law?
15. What was a caul?
16. What stone was used as the second (2) foundation of the city of New Jerusalem?
17. What was the first (1) city of Europe to be evangelized?
18. What affliction did God bring upon Paul at his conversion?
19. What does Solomon say is the beginning of wisdom?
20. What book is known as "The Book of the Beginnings"?

Quiz #4

1. What was the ark of Moses covered with?
2. What did the Lord command Moses to do immediately after he had finished his work?

WHO? WHAT? WHERE? BIBLE QUIZ

3. What special command was given to Israel at the destruction of Jericho?
4. What was the name of the oak near Bethel under which Deborah, Rebekah's nurse was buried?
5. What was the title of the patron God of Babylon?
6. What does Belial mean?
7. What are bellows?
8. What name was given to Daniel by the prince of the Babylonian eunuchs?
9. What name did Jacob give to the child that Rachel named Ben-omi?
10. What was the hometown of Mary, Martha and Lazarus?
11. What hand was the bow of the archer held in?
12. What was the name of the eighth (8) month of the Jewish year?
13. What epithets is used to distinguish Simon the apostle from Peter?
14. What castle did David take for his residence that was later called the city of David?
15. What was a centurion?
16. What stone was used for the third (3) foundation of the wall of the New Jerusalem?
17. What was another name used for the Sea of Galilee?
18. What river flowed out of the Garden of Eden which compassed the whole land of Havilah?
19. What was the Hebrew name of the pavement where Pilate sat down as Jesus was led to him?
20. What great trial did Hannah have?

Quiz #5

1. What does the word "Rabbi" mean?
2. What does "Cephas" mean?
3. What was the name of the wife who was found beside a well?

WHO? WHAT? WHERE? BIBLE QUIZ

4. What is done with unfruitful branches?
5. What was Noah's first act when he departed from the ark?
6. What was Joshua's first commission?
7. What is the Hebrew name of the angel of the bottomless pit?
8. What was the name of the pool at Jerusalem near the sheep gate, which had five porches and was supposed to possess healing virtue?
9. What stone was used for the fourth (4) foundation of the wall of the city of the New Jerusalem?
10. What two (2) kings of Midian did Gibeon pursue and kill?
11. What was the unicorn?
12. What two aspects of Saul's temperament is noticeable in his life?
13. What is the Hebrew counterpart of the Roman and Greek underworld of departed spirits, Hades?
14. What river flowed out of the Garden of Eden which compassed the whole land of Ethiopia?
15. What did the spies who went to Canaan look like in the eyes of the giants?
16. What book was the Ethiopian eunuch reading from when Philip joined himself to the chariot?
17. What material was used to make the Jewish priests garments?
18. What group did Paul belong to before his conversion?
19. What was the result of the death of Gedaliah?
20. What was the results of Jonah's preaching in Ninevah?

Quiz #6

1. What prophet was fed by the ravens?
2. What was Gideon's first act of faith?
3. What was done on the first (1) day of creation?
4. What was created on the second (2) day of creation?
5. What was created on the third (3) day of creation?
6. What was created on the fourth (4) day of creation?

WHO? WHAT? WHERE? BIBLE QUIZ

7. What was created on the fifth (5) day of creation?
8. What was created on the sixth (6) day of creation?
9. What did God do on the seventh (7) day of creation?
10. What is another name for Gideon?
11. What was the chief physical difference between Esau and Jacob?
12. What pleasing traits of character was David always remarkable for?
13. What multilation did the tribe of Judah inflict on Adonibezek?
14. What is a alamoth?
15. What stone was used as the fifth (5) foundation of the wall of the New Jerusalem?
16. What is theophany?
17. What did Samson use to slay one thousand (1,000) Philistines?
18. What three verses of the New Testament contain the term paradise?
19. What kind of bird did Noah release from the ark which flew back and forth until the flood waters abated?
20. What influential deity of Syria did Naaman worship before he was cured of leprosy by the Hebrew prophet Elisha?

Quiz #7

1. What did the king do to Shadrach, Meshach and Abednego?
2. What did the devil promise Eve when he tempted her?
3. What is the meaning of Aceldama?
4. What office did Potiphar appoint Joseph to fill in Egypt?
5. What did God command the Israelites to do before he brought the last plague on the Egyptians?
6. What stone was used for the sixth (6) foundation of the wall of the city of the New Jerusalem?
7. What cliff did the Moabites and Ammonites ascend from En-gedi toward the wilderness of Jeruel and Tekoa?

WHO? WHAT? WHERE? BIBLE QUIZ

8. What was the three (3) departments of knowledge among the Hebrews?
9. What was a wizard?
10. What was the vine of Sodom?
11. What two (2) men did Gamaliel refer to in addressing the Sanhedrin during the arrest of the Apostles as examples of work that came to naught because their deeds were evil and they were not doing the will of God?
12. What Apostle is known as the doubting Apostle?
13. What were the names of the two (2) sons of Simon of Cyrene?
14. What popular form of jewelry was worn by gentlemen in Bible times?
15. What is the secret name of Babylon?
16. What was the Jewish name of queen Esther?
17. What did Samuel's mother bring him every year when she came to offer the yearly sacrifice?
18. What did Jael give to Sisera when he asked for water?
19. What are wisdom's ways called in Proverbs?
20. What book of the Bible is known as the song book of the Hebrews?

Quiz #8

1. What was the name of the tower which was supposed to reach up to heaven?
2. What animals were used for burnt offerings?
3. What did Shamgar, the third judge of Israel, use to kill six hundred (600) Philistine men?
4. What solemn rite did Moses neglect to perform on his son in Midian?
5. What loss did Saul sustain when the Spirit of the Lord rested upon David?
6. What is the Greek name of the angel of the bottomless pit?

7. What stone was used as the seventh (7) foundation of the wall of the city of New Jerusalem?
8. What was vinegar?
9. What was the name of the stone which Samuel set up to commemorate a victory of Israel over the Philistines?
10. What was the seaport for the town of Ephesus?
11. What name did Abraham give to the place where the ram appeared in the thicket?
12. What did Jeremiah say about the condition of the heart?
13. What was the food of John the Baptist in the wilderness?
14. What was the chief city of Macedonia?
15. What did God prepare to kill the gourd which he had held over Jonah which was a shadow over his head?
16. What did the lame man at the gate of the temple which is called "Beautiful" ask of Peter and John?
17. What did the prodigal son eat while he was feeding swine in the far country?
18. What is the meaning of the term "Ecclesiastes"?
19. What remarkable vision did Ezekiel see in chapter 37?
20. What is the subject of the prophecy of Obadiah?

Quiz #9

1. What did God use to cloth Adam and Eve?
2. What is the name of the prophetic battlefield when the kings of the whole world gather together to war of the great day of God?
3. What stone was used as the eighth (8) foundation of the city of the New Jerusalem?
4. What was the occupation of Andrew and Peter?
5. What happened to Nebuchadnezzar when he was driven out from men?
6. What is the theme of the Book of Romans?

7. What gifts did the wise men bring to Jesus?
8. What did Reuben find in the field during the wheat harvest which he brought to his mother?
9. What signs did Thomas require before he would believe in the resurrection of Jesus?
10. What advice did Paul give to Titus as a minister?
11. What was Sarah's reaction when she heard that she was to have a son in her old age?
12. What church did Paul commend because its faith was spoken of throughout the whole world?
13. What was conies?
14. What animal was set apart as the heave of the guilt of the people?
15. What king of the Old Testament ate grass like an ox?
16. What miracle of destruction did Jesus work?
17. What did Abraham give to Hagar and her son when he cast them into the wilderness?
18. What is meant by Anthiopomorphian?
19. What kind of leaf did the dove pluck when it returned to the ark?
20. What was Jacob's name after God changed it?

Quiz #10

1. What great event happened in the days of Peleg?
2. What did the Lord direct Samuel to do to avoid the anger of Saul when he went to Bethlehem to anoint David as king?
3. What was the name of the first city built?
4. What punishment did Moses and Aaron bring upon themselves by not obeying God?
5. What material was the cruse made of which Jesus was anointed with at Bethany?
6. What should a person put on that he may be able to stand against the wiles of the devil?

WHO? WHAT? WHERE? BIBLE QUIZ

7. What stone was used as the ninth (9) foundation of the wall of the city of New Jerusalem?
8. What bird was a herald of Palestinian spring, which arrived about April?
9. What three (3) towns were on the circuit of Samuel which he visited each year?
10. What does the term "coals of fire" on an enemy's head mean?
11. What name did Moses give to the altar he erected after defeating the Amalekites?
12. What was James and John doing when Jesus called them to follow him?
13. What was the theme of John the Baptist's preaching?
14. What vow did Jepthah make to the Lord which forced him to offer his daughter to the Lord for a burnt offering?
15. What did Gideon use to see if God would save Israel by his hand?
16. What affliction did Jesus heal Peter's mother-in-law from?
17. What did Jeremiah predict that the Hinnon valley would be called?
18. What is the annunciation?
19. What did Jacob make for his beloved son, Joseph?
20. What is the wages of sin?

Quiz #11

1. What was used for fuel in the lamps of the tabernacle?
2. What stone was used as the tenth (10) foundation of the wall of the city of the New Jesusalem?
3. What kind of tree did Zacchaeus climb to enable him to see Jesus?
4. What reptile and bird was to be offered for the purification of woman after childbirth and of men whose Nazarite vow had been broken?

WHO? WHAT? WHERE? BIBLE QUIZ

5. What is the gift of God?
6. What was the weakness of Samson's moral fiber?
7. What was the Sanhedrin?
8. What city asked Saul for help when they were beseiged by the Amorites?
9. What was the favorite meat dish of Isaac?
10. What does the Senate of the children of Israel in Acts 5:21 refer to?
11. What was the name of the two (2) well-known crags in the Michmash pass?
12. What name did the prince of the eunuchs give to Hananiah?
13. What was the symbolic name given by Isaiah to his elder son?
14. What was an oracle?
15. What Apostle's name always comes first in the listing of the Apostles?
16. What two (2) men did Paul accuse of teaching an erroneous and upsetting interpretation of the resurrection of believers?
17. What did Ebedmelech use to make the cord with which he drew the prophet Jeremiah out of the dungeon?
18. What country was described as "flowing with milk and honey"?
19. What is an infidel?
20. What was Matthew doing when Jesus called him to follow Him?

Quiz #12

1. What stone was used as the eleventh (11) foundation of the wall of the city of New Jerusalem?
2. What desire did Gideon request of the men of Israel before he would agree to rule over them?
3. What name was given to Joseph by Pharaoh?
4. What did the Philistines do with the body of Saul and his three (3) sons after they had died in Mt. Gilboa?
5. What animals did Elisha use to plow his fields?

6. What two (2) animals was it unlawful to plow with together?
7. What is the only verse in the Bible which contains the name "holy land"?
8. What city was known as the "city of palm trees"?
9. What name is applied to the first (1) five (5) books of the Old Testament?
10. What three (3) apostles were from the same town, Bethsaida?
11. What bird was providentially supplied to hungry Israel on their trek from Egypt toward Canaan?
12. What was the name of the well dug by Isaac's servants named because of the oath made with Abimelech which became the city of Beer-sheba?
13. What jewelry did Aaron melt to make the golden calf?
14. What four (4) requirements did James give before the Jerusalem council for entrance into Christian groups?
15. What mountain was cursed by David in a lament for the loss of Jonathan and his kin?
16. Who were the Grecians?
17. What caused Nabal's death?
18. What event occurred that released Paul and Silas from prison as they prayed and sang praises to God?
19. What is the moral of the Song of Solomon?
20. What Old Testament prophet is quoted more than any other in the New Testament?

Quiz #13

1. What stone was used as the twelveth (12) foundation of the wall of the city of New Jerusalem?
2. What name did Nebuchadnezzar give to Mattaniah on appointing him vassal-king of Judah?
3. What was the promise given to Shem for his loyalty to his father in the latter's sin after the flood?

WHO? WHAT? WHERE? BIBLE QUIZ

4. What was an oblation?
5. What word did Jephthah use to test whether the fugitives were Ephraimites or Gileadites?
6. What jewelry did Abraham's servant give to Rebekah at the well?
7. What is another name that is used interchangeably for the country of Edom?
8. What original language was the New Testament written in?
9. What original language was the Old Testament written in?
10. What was carried from Paul to the sick that had the power of miraculous cure?
11. What does the term "that someone's blood was upon the head" mean?
12. What did Solomon ask for when he prayed for the greatest gift that he could think of?
13. What was another name for Hebron where Sarah died?
14. What did the people of Lystra call Barnabas?
15. What term is used to indicate the first (1) six (6) books of the Old Testament?
16. What is to be done with a tree which does not yield good fruit?
17. What plant was used in observance of the passover?
18. What did God call "Sarai" after he had changed her name?
19. What theme did Stephen preach when he was brought before the council?
20. What was Moses doing when he had the vision of the burning bush?

Quiz #14

1. What was the twelve (12) gates of the city of New Jerusalem made of?
2. What was the streets of the city of New Jerusalem made of?
3. What animal was it unlawful to muzzle when he treadeth out the corn?

4. What trees were symbolic of prosperity?
5. What other name does Isaiah give to Jerusalem?
6. What did the people of Lystra call Paul?
7. What king of Judah initiated a series of reforms that eliminated certain Canaanitish serpent-fertility rites and idolatrous Jewish cults?
8. What was another name of Dorcas whom Peter raised from the dead?
9. What river did Lot look over and choose all the lands which this river watered?
10. What year was celebrated as the Jubilee year?
11. What highway did Moses desire to use to lead Israel through Edom?
12. What were the physical disqualifications of a priest under the Mosaic law?
13. What does the writer of Proverbs compare the putting out of a flame to?
14. What were the lavers of the Tabernacle and Temple made of?
15. What was the duty of the Levites?
16. What natural act accompanied the appearance of God to Moses on Mt. Sinai?
17. What two (2) churches of Macedonia did Paul write Epistles to?
18. What name did Isaiah write in a public place and later gave his second (2) son as a sign that Syria and Israel would soon be conquered by Assyria?
19. What name did Naomi apply to herself after the death of her husband and sons?
20. What sin did Jesus say would not be forgiven?

Quiz #15

1. What reward was Ebedmelech promised for drawing the prophet Jeremiah out of a dungeon by a cord?

WHO? WHAT? WHERE? BIBLE QUIZ

2. What is faith?
3. What did the writer of Proverbs say would exalt a nation?
4. What was the spiritual condition of the people who lived in Sodom and Gomorrah?
5. What happened to the men who had Daniel thrown into the lion's den?
6. What did Paul say that he would not eat if it caused others to be offended?
7. What sins of Israel does Micah enumerate?
8. What king of Judah reigned only one (1) month?
9. What church was known as the dead church in Revelations?
10. What church was known as the luke warm church in Revelations?
11. What advantage did the Jews have over other nations?
12. What was the central theme of Paul's preaching?
13. What was the food of John the Baptist?
14. What did David tell Solomon to do at his death?
15. What did the widows show Peter after Dorcas' death?
16. What saved Balaam's life three (3) times when the angel of the Lord stood in the way?
17. What large city did Paul preach in that he never mentioned in any of his writings?
18. What did the two (2) blind men at Jericho cry out to Jesus as he passed by?
19. What hindered the progress of the church at Galatia?
20. What did God send to help Joshua in defeating the Amorites at Beth-horon?

Quiz #16

1. What community was formed by the descendents of Caleb and his wife Ephrath?
2. What city was cited by the Assyrians as an example of the futility of offering resistance to Assyria?

WHO? WHAT? WHERE? BIBLE QUIZ

3. What meat dish did the scheming Rebekah substitute for Isaac's favorite dish of venison?
4. What was a scepter?
5. What is a schism?
6. What name did the prince of the eunuchs give to Michael?
7. What river did Ehud seize the Moabite fords in?
8. What church accepted a wicked woman as pastor?
9. What was the gospel of Christ to the Jews?
10. What did John see through the open door of heaven?
11. What did Hannah promise the Lord if she should be given a male child?
12. What teaching does the book of James present?
13. What was the nationality of Titus?
14. What are the general epistles?
15. What king made presents to David?
16. What did the Israelites do when they had passed over the Red Sea?
17. What solemn rite did Joshua renew at Gilgal?
18. What animal did Christ use to make his triumphal entry into Jerusalem?
19. What three (3) cities did Jesus denounce for their unbelief?
20. What was the name given to Palestine after the exile, when it was repeopled and restored to God's favor?

Quiz #17

1. What message did Joab send to David?
2. What three (3) cities did Moses establish where men who had killed their neighbors accidently might find refuge?
3. What three (3) languages was the superscription "This is the Kings of the Jews" written in on the cross?
4. What title did Jesus bestow upon James and John?

WHO? WHAT? WHERE? BIBLE QUIZ

5. What was the chief industry of Bozrah, home of King Jobab of Edom?
6. What city was called Jesus' own city?
7. What was the national diety of Moab to whom living children were sacrificed by burning?
8. What city did Pharaoh burn and then presented it as a gift to Solomon's wife?
9. What is a Corban?
10. What Aegean island did Paul spend one (1) night at on his way from Miletus to Rhodes on his third (3) missionary journey?
11. What was a cup-bearer?
12. What did Darius find in the palace at Achmetha?
13. What was the occupation of Demetrius of Ephesus?
14. What is meant by "Abraham's Bosom"?
15. What did God set in the cloud as a token to Noah that a second (2) deluge would not destroy all flesh?
16. What did Joseph's brethren cast him into?
17. What complaint did the officers of the children of Israel make to Pharaoh?
18. What fuel was used in the lamps in the tabernacle?
19. What nation did the Lord send Saul to destroy?
20. What is repentance?

Quiz #18

1. What town was the hometown of Nathanael?
2. What valley did the Philistines come out of into the wilderness of Judah to threaten Saul and Jonathan?
3. What was the duties of the scribes?
4. What name did the prince of the eunuchs give to Azariah?
5. What is the present name of the country of Persia of the Bible?
6. What was a Pestle?

WHO? WHAT? WHERE? BIBLE QUIZ

7. What brought about the friendship between Pilate and Herod?
8. What does the words "Eli Eli lamb Sabachthani" which Christ cried from the cross mean?
9. What reward did the woman of Shunem receive for her hospitality to Elisha?
10. What was the name of the tempestuous wind that arose against Paul's ship when he was sailing to Crete on the way to Rome?
11. What did Saul do with those that had familiar spirits and the wizards?
12. What was an ephod?
13. What kind of wood did God command Noah to build his ark of?
14. What four (4) New Testament books are known as the gospels?
15. What two (2) objections did Moses advance when God commissioned him?
16. What did Paul say about the throat of the unbelieving Jew?
17. What was the gospel of Christ to the Greeks?
18. What does Jesus compare the kingdom to in the parable of the labours in the vineyard?
19. What was the name of the son that God gave to Adam in the place of Abel, whom Cain slew?
20. What did Potiphar, the Egyptian, do to Joseph after his wife falsely accused him?

WHERE? BIBLE QUIZ

INTRODUCTION

How well do you know Bible Geography? How readily can you recall where some event of the Bible took place?

These quizzes will help you to learn the location of many of the events of the Bible readily. These quizzes are not intended merely to entertain, but to help you to grasp the full meaning of the Word of God.

If you will take the little time and effort necessary to learn these questions and answers plus the references, you will have a knowledge of the where's of God's word so that you will be able to recall where the event took place.

I hope that you will find this study as enjoyable to master as I found it to prepare.

Good luck and may you be good workmen for Christ, armed with the knowledge of the word.

M. S.

WHO? WHAT? WHERE? BIBLE QUIZ

Quiz #1

1. Where did Barnabas go to seek a helper?
2. Where did the mother of Jesus live after the crucifixion?
3. Where did Jesus attend a wedding?
4. Where did Paul find an altar erected to the unknown God?
5. Where did John write the Book of Revelation?
6. Where is Jesus now?
7. Where did Deborah, the fourth judge of Israel, dwell?
8. Where did Abraham bury Sarah?
9. Where was Solomon's temple built?
10. Where did the tribes assemble to receive Saul as their king?
11. Where did the Lord send Samuel to anoint a king?
12. Where did Paul board the ship for his trip to Rome?
13. Where did Miriam die?
14. Where did Peter heal Aeneas of the palsy?
15. Where did Jeroboam put the two (2) golden calves that he had made?
16. Where was the Judge Elon buried?
17. Where did the Mariners and valiant defenders of the stronghold of Tyre come from in Ezekiel's time?
18. Where was the tower of Babel located?
19. Where did the daughter of Pharoah bathe?
20. Where did the children of Israel dig a well with their staves?

Quiz #2

1. Where was John the Baptist baptizing when the Pharisees questioned him about whether he was the Messiah?
2. Where was Jesus born?
3. Where did Tola, the seventh (7) judge of Israel live?
4. Where in the land of Egypt did Jacob and his family dwell?
5. Where did the angel Gabriel appear to Zacharias?
6. Where was David when he sent Joab to beseige Rabbah?

WHO? WHAT? WHERE? BIBLE QUIZ

7. Where was the palace of king Ahasuerus?
8. Where was Achan stoned to death?
9. Where was Deborah, Rebekah's nurse buried?
10. Where was Paul met by Christians from Rome when he was being brought a prisoner to the capitol?
11. Where was Solomon's vineyard which he let out to keepers for a thousand (1,000) pieces of silver from each?
12. Where did Hagar learn that Jehovah watched over her?
13. Where did Abraham make a covenant with Abimelech?
14. Where did Rachel die?
15. Where was the pool of Bethesda?
16. Where is the life of the flesh?
17. Where did the Israelites repent and weep under the rebuke of the angel of the Lord for their disobedience of God's commands?
18. Where was the bones of Saul and Jonathan buried?
19. Where was Daniel when he saw the prophetic ram and the goats in a vision?
20. Where was Rachel buried?

Quiz #3

1. Where was Jesus taken by his parents when he was just a few days old?
2. Where was Abraham born?
3. Where was Jesus taken on a visit when he was twelve (12) years old?
4. Where was Ibzan, the tenth (10) judge, born and buried?
5. Where did Joshua make his solemn covenant with Israel before his death?
6. Where was the residence of Ruth?
7. Where was Phebe a servant in the church?
8. Where did Jesus meet Zacchaeus?

WHO? WHAT? WHERE? BIBLE QUIZ

9. Where did Saul receive a sign of his royalty from the Lord after his anointing by Samuel the prophet?
10. Where did Paul continue to preach in Ephesus after he was expelled from the synagogue?
11. Where did Jacob hide all the strange gods and earrings which the people had given him?
12. Where did Joseph's father-in-law serve as a priest?
13. Where did Isaac and Jacob obtain their wives, Rebekah and Rachel?
14. Where was the home of the apostles, Philip, Andrew and Peter?
15. Where did the five (5) kings hide whom Joshua pursued and finally killed?
16. Where did Balak erect seven (7) altars of sacrifice?
17. Where did the Lord reveal Himself to Samuel?
18. Where did the Israelites fight the giant king Og and kill him?
19. Where was Jesus anointed by Mary with precious ointment?
20. Where was Paul when he was bitten by a venomous serpent?

Quiz #4

1. Where was Solomon's porch located?
2. Where did Mary, Martha and Lazarus live?
3. Where were the followers of Christ first called Christians?
4. Where was Moses buried?
5. Where did Cornelius, a centurion of the Italian band, live?
6. Where did Christ receive a royal welcome?
7. Where did Paul make his decision to turn from the Jews to the Gentiles?
8. Where did the fire of the Lord burn the people of Israel?
9. Where did the angel of the Lord appear to Samson's father?
10. Where did the wise men seek the infant Jesus?
11. Where did Jephthah flee where he lived as an outlaw?

WHO? WHAT? WHERE? BIBLE QUIZ

12. Where was the bones of Joseph buried after the children of Israel brought them out of Egypt?
13. Where did the people in Isaiah's and Jeremiah's time sacrifice their children by burning them in idolatrous rites sacred to Molech?
14. Where did Lydia, the seller of purple, live?
15. Where did the Lord confound the languages of all the earth?
16. Where did Jesus heal the man sick with palsy?
17. Where was the apostle John when he received his great vision?
18. Where was Paul when the prophet Agabus warned him not to go to Jerusalem?
19. Where was Saul crowned king?
20. Where was Goliath's brother slain?

Quiz #5

1. Where did Jesus spend His boyhood?
2. Where did Mary and Martha meet Jesus at the time of the death of Lazarus?
3. Where did Jacob first meet Rachel?
4. Where was Barak when Deborah called him to be the fifth (5) judge of Israel?
5. Where did Ibzan, the tenth (10) judge of Israel, get the thirty (30) wives for his thirty (30) sons?
6. Where did Moses flee after he killed the Egyptian?
7. Where did Paul and Barnabas depart from on their first missionary journey?
8. Where did Noah's ark come to rest?
9. Where did the man come from who brought bread and corn of the first fruit to Elisha from which he miraculously fed a hundred (100) men?
10. Where did Jehoshaphat lose his fleet when he attempted to duplicate the gold-buying projects of Solomon?

WHO? WHAT? WHERE? BIBLE QUIZ

11. Where did John Mark separate from Paul and Barnabas to return to Jerusalem?
12. Where was the god Baal-zebub consulted by agents of King Ahaziah?
13. Where did Ishmael and his men kill Gedaliah?
14. Where did the children of Israel bury the people that lusted after the quail?
15. Where did Mephibosheth, Jonathan's lame son, live before he was summoned by David to his court?
16. Where did Ezekiel see visions of God?
17. Where did Job live?
18. Where did Jonah flee to when the Lord told him to go to the city of Ninevah?
19. Where did Jesus walk on the first (1) easter afternoon when he met two (2) of his disciples?
20. Where did Jesus ordain the twelve (12) apostles?

Quiz #6

1. Where did Mary and Joseph go to pay tribute when Jesus was born?
2. Where did God put man when he was created?
3. Where were all the first (1) born slain at midnight?
4. Where did Paul and Barnabas meet the proconsul, Segius Paulus, who called for them to hear the "word of God"?
5. Where did Elimelich and his family flee during the famine in Bethlehem?
6. Where did the people believe Paul and Barnabas were gods and the local priests tried to offer a sacrifice to them?
7. Where was Moses born?
8. Where did Jesus meet the woman of Samaria?
9. Where did Jonathan hide when he learned that Absalom sought to kill him?

10. Where was Christ when he ascended to heaven?
11. Where did Paul visit the disciples for seven (7) days while his ship was being unloaded?
12. Where did Ezra, the scribe, live before he returned to Jerusalem?
13. Where was the first (1) prayer meeting held?
14. Where did Paul minister in Thessalonica?
15. Where was Paul when a viper came out of the heat and fastened itself upon his hand?
16. Where did the Lord appear unto Abraham as he sat in the door of the tents in the heat of the day?
17. Where did the Lord set Ezekiel down?
18. Where was Christ crucified?
19. Where did Daniel see himself in a vision?
20. Where did Aaron die?

Quiz #7

1. Where did Terah die?
2. Where was Jesus baptized?
3. Where did Jabin reign as king?
4. Where was Abimelech born?
5. Where did Elijah raise the widow's son to life?
6. Where was the apostle Paul born?
7. Where did the midnight arrest of Jesus take place?
8. Where was the early home of Saul?
9. Where did Apollos learn the way of God more perfectly?
10. Where did Jesus tell the man who was born blind to go and wash?
11. Where was Elijah when he was taken up into heaven?
12. Where did Abram first settle after he left Haran?
13. Where did Jesus weep over a city?
14. Where should we lay up our treasures?

WHO? WHAT? WHERE? BIBLE QUIZ

15. Where did Paul go when he returned from Arabia?
16. Where did Rachel hide her father's images which she had stolen?
17. Where did Rahab hide the spies?
18. Where did Joshua rear the tabernacle and at his death make a covenant with Israel?
19. Where did Ezra assemble the Jews to prepare them spiritually for their journey out of Babylonian captivity back to Jerusalem?
20. Where was the house of Ashtaroh located?

Quiz #8

1. Where did the brethen send Saul from Jerusalem?
2. Where did Abram go to avoid a famine in his homeland?
3. Where was Abdon, the twelvth (12) judge of Israel, buried?
4. Where was Elijah miraculously fed by ravens?
5. Where did Abraham lie to Abimelech in telling him that Sarah was his sister?
6. Where did Solomon obtain much of his gold and other wealth which Hiram brought to him?
7. Where did the vengeful hanging of Saul's seven sons take place?
8. Where did the Israelites hide when the Midianites invaded their homeland?
9. Where did David go into the house of the Lord, and take and eat of the holy bread?
10. Where was John the Baptist beheaded?
11. Where did Jeremiah die?
12. Where did Paul go after his conversion?
13. Where did Absalom flee to after he murdered his brother Ammon?
14. Where did Jesus heal Peter's mother-in-law?
15. Where did Melchizedek live?

WHO? WHAT? WHERE? BIBLE QUIZ

16. Where did Christ send his disciples to get the ass on which he made his triumphal entry into Jerusalem?
17. Where did Paul's ship find shelter from rough weather during his trip to Rome?
18. Where did the Israelites lose the ark to the Philistines?
19. Where did Abimelech reign as king?
20. Where was Abraham when he entertained three (3) men?

Quiz #9

1. Where did Peter go when he was released from prison?
2. Where did Abraham live before he lived in Charran?
3. Where was Jair, the eighth (8) judge of Israel, buried?
4. Where did Paul withstand Peter face to face because of his vacillating conduct with regard to the gentile converts?
5. Where did Jesus withdraw upon hearing the news of the murder of John the Baptist?
6. Where was Pekahiah when he was assassinated?
7. Where did Paul and Barnabas go on their first missionary journey, when they were expelled from Antioch by the opposition of the Jewish people?
8. Where did Rahab live?
9. Where did Moses receive his education?
10. Where does Abaddon and Apollyon rule?
11. Where did Lot and his two (2) daughters go from Zoar because he feared to dwell in Zoar?
12. Where did the fugitive David hide in a cave?
13. Where was the prophet Jeremiah born?
14. Where did Paul meet Timothy?
15. Where did the descendants of Jacob mourn for seven (7) days on their journey from Egypt with Jacob's body to his burial place at Hebron?
16. Where did the Israelites assemble to make Rehoboam king?

17. Where did Lot and his two (2) daughters flee when Sodom was destroyed?
18. Where did Mary go after the angel announced to her that Jesus was to be born?
19. Where did Jeroboam establish his capital?
20. Where was Jehoshaphat buried?

Quiz #10

1. Where did Saul go after he left Damascus?
2. Where was Jephthah living when he was called to be the ninth (9) judge of Israel, and he lead the army against the children of Ammon?
3. Where was David when the news came to him of the death of Saul and Jonathan?
4. Where did Samuel build an altar to the Lord?
5. Where was the home of Gideon?
6. Where had Jesus seen Nathanael before Philip introduced them?
7. Where was Gideon when the angel of the Lord appeared to him to call him as judge?
8. Where did Samson find a swarm of bees?
9. Where did Peter and John heal the man who was lame from his mother's womb?
10. Where did Micah live?
11. Where did the brethren send Paul and Silas to escape the persecution of the unbelieving Jews in Thessalonica?
12. Where was Benjamin named?
13. Where did Jesus go when he heard that John the Baptist was in prison?
14. Where did Barnabas and John Mark go when they separated from Paul?
15. Where did Ezra proclaim a fast to ask God to protect him from danger on his journey to Jerusalem?

16. Where was Joshua buried?
17. Where did Nabal engage in sheep-raising?
18. Where did Jesus and his disciples go after the feeding of the four thousand (4,000)?
19. Where was Aaron buried?
20. Where was the bodies of Saul and his three (3) sons fastened to the city wall?

Quiz #11

1. Where did the trial of Paul before Festus and Agrippa take place?
2. Where did the conversation between Jesus and Peter arising out of the question "Who do men say that I am" take place?
3. Where did Paul's friends meet him and hold a prayer-meeting on the seashore?
4. Where did Samuel serve Eli the priest?
5. Where did Saul and his three (3) sons die?
6. Where did King Chedorlaomer of Sodom meet Abraham as he returned from rescuing his nephew Lot?
7. Where did Elijah and Ahab meet to discuss the merits of Jehovah versus Baal?
8. Where did Ishmael flee with his mother, Hagar, when they were banished from his father Abraham's encampment?
9. Where did Jacob wrestle with a stranger and receive an angelic blessing?
10. Where does John say that the seat of Satan is?
11. Where did Philemon live?
12. Where was Manasseh carried captive because of his idolatrous worship?
13. Where did Gideon and his men conceal their torches?
14. Where did Joshua cast lots for the assignment of territory to the various tribes?

15. Where did Joshua build an altar, erected stones inscribed with the law and pronounced to Israel the curses for the breach of the law?
16. Where did David kill the giant Goliath?
17. Where did Peter raise Dorcas from the dead?
18. Where did Tiglath-pileser deport the Aramaeans from Damascus?
19. Where was Nebuchadnezzar king?
20. Where did Absalom flee to after he killed his half-brother Ammon?

Quiz #12

1. Where did the angel of the Lord appear to Hagar?
2. Where did Manoah, the father of Samson, live?
3. Where was the temple of Diana located?
4. Where did Moses hide the Egyptian whom he had killed?
5. Where did Jonah flee to try to escape the presence of the Lord?
6. Where did Naomi bring her two (2) daughters-in-law after leaving Moab?
7. Where did Solomon banish Abiathai to for suspected treachery?
8. Where was Moses when God gave him the instructions about sacrifices?
9. Where was the fire obtained to burn the sacrifice and the incense in the tabernacle?
10. Where will the final contest between the forces of good and evil ultimately take place?
11. Where did Paul meet Lydia?
12. Where did Jesus cure the blind beggar, Bartimaeus?
13. Where was the army of Ben-hadad defeated?
14. Where did Abraham build his first Palestinian altar?
15. Where did Samson slay a thousand (1,000) Philistines with the jawbone of an ass?

WHO? WHAT? WHERE? BIBLE QUIZ

16. Where did the Philistines put the armour of Saul after he killed himself?
17. Where did Saul set up a monument to commemorate his victory over the Amalekites?
18. Where was Abram living when God called him?
19. Where was Jesus unable to do any mighty works?
20. Where was Eleazar buried?

Quiz #13

1. Where did Elisha purify the poisonous pottage?
2. Where did the family of Moses's father-in-law settle after the death of Joshua?
3. Where was Sennacherib when his two (2) sons killed him?
4. Where did the Assyrians transport the people from to replace the captives taken from Samaria?
5. Where must the strength of the Christian be when he goes against his spiritual enemies?
6. Where did Joshua issue his challenge to the sun and moon?
7. Where did Hagar get her son's wife?
8. Where did Agabus make his prediction of a famine and also the binding of Paul?
9. Where was John the Baptist before he began his public ministry?
10. Where did John the Baptist baptize in Judaea?
11. Where did Ruth live after the famine?
12. Where was the hometown of Nathaniel, Jesus' apostle?
13. Where did the sons of Sennacherib flee after killing their father at worship?
14. Where was the city court known as the Areopagus located before whom Paul was heard?
15. Where was Aquila born?
16. Where was the ark of God taken into the Temple of Dagon?
17. Where was Mars Hill located?

WHO? WHAT? WHERE? BIBLE QUIZ

18. Where did David first observe Bath-sheba?
19. Where did David's servants stay until their beards regrew after Hanun had shaved half of them off?
20. Where did Ben-hadad live when he was bribed by Asa to attack Baashua?

Quiz #14

1. Where did the council of chief priests, scribes and elders take place to devise measures for the arrest of Christ?
2. Where was the servant of Elijah when he saw a little cloud arise out of the sea like a man's hand?
3. Where did Paul and Barnabas embark for Cyprus on the first (1) missionary journey?
4. Where did Jesus often go at evening when the men went to their homes?
5. Where did the remnants of the Benjaminites hide in the vineyards and capture girls for marriage who were dancing among the vines?
6. Where did Samuel set up the stone Ebenezer to commemorate a victory of Israel over the Philistines?
7. Where was the oasis of (70) seventy palm trees and (12) wells of water where the children of Israel encamped?
8. Where was the angel Gabriel's abode?
9. Where did Jesus heal the man with an unclean spirit?
10. Where did the children of Israel strip themselves of their ornaments?
11. Where was Paul stoned and left on the outside of the city for dead?
12. Where was Jacob's well located?
13. Where did Peter make his confession of Jesus as "the Christ, the son of the living God"?
14. Where did God command Jonah to go to preach which he refused to do, but afterwards repented and obeyed?

WHO? WHAT? WHERE? BIBLE QUIZ

15. Where did Lot live after he separated from Abraham?
16. Where was Jesus when he was mistaken for a ghost or spirit?
17. Where did Jesus go after His temptation?
18. Where did Nicodemus come to Jesus by night?
19. Where did God say that he would meet his people?
20. Where did Belshazzar reign as king?

Quiz #15

1. Where did Ahasuerus reign?
2. Where does the broad way and the wide gate of Matt. 7:13 lead to?
3. Where did King Asa cut down his mother's idol and burn it?
4. Where was Paul baptized?
5. Where was Paul when he wrote his epistle to the Phillipians?
6. Where was Jesus when he healed the ear of Malchus, the high priest's servant?
7. Where did Nebuchadnezzar set up the golden image in Babylon?
8. Where did Joshua pronounce to assembled Israel the curses that would follow breaches of the law?
9. Where did Jesus go after his baptism?
10. Where was Bethany in relation to Jerusalem?
11. Where did Samson put the gates of Gaza when he carried them away?
12. Where were the cities of refuge built by Moses to shelter anyone who had accidentally killed another?
13. Where did Samson get the thirty (30) garments to pay the Philistines for expounding his riddle?
14. Where did the conspiracy of Abimelech to be king take place?
15. Where did Samson kill a young lion with his bare hands?
16. Where did Elimelech and Naomi live before they went to sojourn in Moab?
17. Where were the castings for Solomon's temple made?

WHO? WHAT? WHERE? BIBLE QUIZ

18. Where did God tell Elijah to go when the brook Cherith dried up?
19. Where was king Joram returned to be healed of the wounds which the Syrians had given him when he fought with Hazael, king of Syria?
20. Where was Ahaz buried?

Quiz #16

1. Where was the herdsman — prophet, Amos, born?
2. Where did Aaron and Hur hold up Moses praying hands while Joshua won the battle between the Israelites and the nomadic Amalekites?
3. Where did Jesus heal the "two (2) demoniacs"?
4. Where did Solomon form his navy?
5. Where was Abraham directed to offer his son, Isaac, as a burnt offering?
6. Where does the narrow way and the strait gate of Matt. 7:14 lead to?
7. Where was Jesus buried?
8. Where did the Shunammite widow go to live to avoid a famine after Elisha had restored her son?
9. Where did Nebuchadnezzar carry Jehoiachin captive?
10. Where was Ezekiel transported to see a glorious temple and the healing waters issuing from it?
11. Where did Jesus heal the man which had an infirmity thirty eight (38) years?
12. Where did Jesus live after his parents returned with Him from Egypt?
13. Where did Israel's forces gather before the battle of Gilboa?
14. Where was Gilgal located?
15. Where did Sennacherib station his army under Rabshekeh to advance toward Jerusalem?

16. Where did Ahaziah flee to and die when he was wounded by Jehu?

17. Where did Joram of Judah encamp before he attacked the Edomites?

18. Where did the spies which Moses sent out cut down grapes, pomegranates and figs as a testimony of the exceeding good land which they were invited to go up and possess?

19. Where was Absalom's headquarters during his rebellion against his father?

20. Where was Abner when he was assassinated by Joab?

Quiz #17

1. Where did David deposit the ark for three (3) months for safe-keeping before transporting it to Jerusalem?

2. Where was Jesus when he pronounced his lament over Jerusalem and the judgment of its people?

3. Where was Moses when he dispatched spies to report on conditions in the land of Canaan?

4. Where did the Egyptian Pharaoh — Nechoh put King Jehoahaz II of Judah in chains and levied heavy tribute on his kingdom?

5. Where did King Saul visit a witch on the eve of the fatal battle of Gilboa?

6. Where was Elisha going when he was mocked by some irreverent little children?

7. Where was Peter ministering when he was called to come to Joppa to raise Dorcas from the dead?

8. Where did Cain dwell after he went out from the presence of the Lord?

9. Where did the Judge Barak live?

10. Where was Naboth's vineyard which Ahab coveted?

11. Where was Ish-basheth, son of Saul, made king by Abner?

12. Where did Isaac's bride originally live?

WHO? WHAT? WHERE? BIBLE QUIZ

13. Where was Jesus betrayed by a kiss?
14. Where did Samson find a harlot whom he went in unto?
15. Where were the Israelites first miraculously fed with quails in answer to their murmurings?
16. Where did the cloud of the Israelites rest after it was taken from off the tabernacle of the testimony?
17. Where was the chariot which brought the body of the slain Ahab to Samaria washed?
18. Where did Joshua see the captain of the host of the Lord with a sword drawn against him?
19. Where was Amasa assassinated?
20. Where did the Lord send hailstones on the retreating army that gave Joshua a great victory?

Quiz #18

1. Where did Jesus use Simon's ship for a pulpit to teach the people?
2. Where did Moses make the golden calf?
3. Where did Jeroboam flee when Solomon sought to kill him?
4. Where was the rich man when he wanted Lazarus to dip the tip of his finger in water and cool his tongue?
5. Where did Jesus go after his night interview with Nicodemus?
6. Where was Daniel spied upon by his enemies?
7. Where did Elijah flee for fear of Jezebel?
8. Where did the Philistines gather their army before the battle of Gilboa?
9. Where did the seventy (70) sons of Ahab live?
10. Where were the eyes of Zedekiah put out after his children had been slain in his sight?
11. Where did David flee to when he was driven from his home by the treason of Absalom?
12. Where did the battle between Barak and Sisera take place?

13. Where was Samuel dedicated to God and spent his childhood?
14. Where did the parents of Jesus find Him when He became separated from them in Jerusalem?
15. Where was Urijah the prophet born?
16. Where did Elisha smite the Syrian army with blindness?
17. Where did Amaziah gain a victory over Edom when he slew ten thousand (10,000) men and took Selah by war?
18. Where did Paul see a light shine from heaven around him?
19. Where was Jesus taken to be presented to the Lord where his circumcision took place?
20. Where did Jesus drive the money changers out of the temple?

WHO? WHAT? WHERE? BIBLE QUIZ — ANSWERS

Quiz #1

1. John. John 1:8
2. James. Mark 1:19
3. James. Acts 12:2
4. Lois. II Tim. 1:5
5. Cain. Genesis 4:8
6. Joseph. Genesis 37:3
7. Eli. I Sam. 4:18
8. Candace. Acts 8:27
9. Paul. Eph. 3:1, 4:1
10. Miriam. Num. 12:10
11. Luke. Col. 4:14
12. Lydia. Acts 16:14
13. James. Acts 12:2
14. Gabriel. Luke 1:30
15. Herodias. Matt. 14:8
16. John Mark. Acts 15:39
17. Mephibosheth. II Sam. 4:4
18. Methuselah. Gen. 5:24-27
19. Michal. I Sam. 19:11, 12
20. Mordecai. Esther 2:7

Quiz #2

1. Moses. John 3:14
2. Barnabas and Saul. Acts 11:30
3. Ruth. Ruth 4:17
4. Peter. Matt. 14:29-30
5. Agrippa. Acts 26:28
6. Vashti. Esther 1:9
7. Sisera. Judges 4:21
8. Othniel. Judges 3:9
9. God's own people. Psalm 1:3 92:12-14
10. David. I Sam. 16:21
11. Isaac. Gen. 25:11
12. Joshua. Josh. 3:17
13. Araunah. II Sam. 24:18-25
14. Obed. II Chron. 28:9-15
15. God. Isa. 30:12, 15
16. Jeroboam. Hosea 1:1
17. Herod. Acts 12:23
18. Paul. Acts 27:21-37
19. Jacob. Gen. 28:10-15
20. King Herod. Luke 13:31-32

Quiz #3

1. Samuel. I Sam. 3:8
2. Gideon. Judges 7:19

3. Nathanael. John 1:47
4. Boaz. Ruth 4:13
5. Joseph of Arimathea. Matt. 27:58-59
6. Ehud. Judges 3:15
7. Joab. II Sam. 18:14
8. Abidan. Num. 2:22
9. Jubal. Gen. 4:21
10. Josiah. Zeph. 1:1
11. The Midianites. Gen. 37:36
12. His mother. Pro. 31:1-4
13. The fool. Psalm 14:1
14. Sisera. Judges 4:7-9
15. Diotrephes. III John 9-10
16. Zechariah. Zech. 5:1-4
17. Joel. Joel 2:28-32
18. Timothy. Acts 16:1-3
19. The Philippian prison-keeper. Acts 16:25-40
20. Pilate's wife. Matt. 27:19

Quiz #4

1. John. Matt. 3:13
2. John. John 19:26; 20:2
3. Elijah. I Kings 18:21-39
4. Zadok. I Kings 1:39
5. Diana. Acts 19:28
6. Joshua. Josh. 3:17
7. Cornelius. Acts 10:1
8. Jesus. John 2:9
9. Shamgar. Judges 3:31
10. Jair. Judges 10:4
11. Zacchaeus. Luke 19:4
12. Bilhah, his father's concubine. Gen. 35:22
13. Uzziah. Amos 1:1
14. King Solomon. I Kings 9:26
15. Adam and Eve. Gen. 3:8
16. Enoch. Jude 14
17. Jonah, Amos, Hosea, Isaiah, Joel, Micah, Nahum, Zephaniah, Jeremiah.
18. Habakkuk, Daniel, Obadiah, Ezekiel.
19. Haggai, Zechariah, Malachi.
20. Ashpenaz. Dan. 1:3

Quiz #5

1. Joshua. Deut. 34:9

71

WHO? WHAT? WHERE? BIBLE QUIZ — ANSWERS

2. Jonathan. I Sam. 20:17
3. Demetrius. Acts 19:24
4. Deborah. Judges 4:4
5. Athaliah. II Kings 11:1:2
6. Felix. Acts 24:24-26
7. Elahanan. II Sam. 21;19
8. James and John. Mark 3:17
9. Caleb and Joshua. Num. 14:6-8
10. Deborah. Judges 4:4
11. Joseph of Arimathae. Matt. 27:60
12. Sherah. I Chron. 7:24
13. Potiphar. Gen. 37:36 ff
14. God. Gen. 3:14
15. Asshur. Gen. 10:11
16. Micah. Micah 1:1
17. Uzziah. II Chron. 26:16-21
18. James, Cephas, John. Gal. 2:9
19. Ithamar and Eleazar. Lev. 10:16-17
20. Samuel. I Sam. 16:7

Quiz #6

1. Daniel. Dan. 6:16
2. Pharaoh. Exodus 14:5
3. Andrew. John 6:9
4. Ahab. I Kings 16:29-33
5. Daniel. Dan. 2:48
6. David. I Sam. 17:49
7. Elijah. II Kings 2:11
8. Elisha. II Kings 4:1-7
9. Dorcas. Acts 9:40
10. Barak. Judges 4:6
11. Ahijah. I Kings 11:29-39
12. Nimrod. Gen. 10:9
13. Nahum. Nahum 1:1
14. Peter. Acts 4:1-4; 12:1-4
15. Elijah and Elisha. II Kings 2:1-5
16. Pontius Pilate. John 18:31
17. Silas. Acts 16:25-26
18. Thomas. John 20:24
19. Titus. Titus 1:5
20. Caleb. Joshua 15:14

Quiz #7

1. Pilate. Luke 23:1
2. Noah. Gen. 6:22
3. Nathanael. John 1:48
4. The devil. John 8:44
5. Joash. II Kings 12:4-16

6. Jeroboam. I Kings 11:40
7. Gamaliel. Acts 22:3
8. Balaam. Num. 22:33
9. Gideon. Judges 6:14
10. Ahikam. Jer. 26:24
11. Elnathan. Jer. 26:22
12. Uzzah and Ahio. II Sam. 6:3,4
13. Nathanael. John 1:46
14. His wives. I Kings 11:3
15. Jonah because he refused at first to go to Ninevah at the command of God.
16. Naboth. I Kings 21:9-15
17. Nicodemus. John 19:39
18. Abaddon. Rev. 9:11
19. Naaman. II Kings 5:1
20. Barabbas. Luke 23:19

Quiz #8

1. Judas. John 18:5
2. Abraham. Gen. 22:10
3. Paul. Acts. 9:3
4. Eutychus. Acts 20:7-12
5. Jehosheba. II Kings 11:2
6. Barnabas. Acts 4:37
7. Bartimaeus. Mark 10:46-52
8. Tola. Judges 10:1
9. Deborah. Gen. 35:8
10. Apollyon. Rev. 9:11
11. Philip the evangelist. Acts 21:9
12. Reuben. Gen. 42:36-38
13. Ebedmelech. Jer. 38:11
14. Elijah. I Kings 18:17-40
15. Eli. I Sam. 3:12, 13
16. Peter and John. Acts 3:1, 4:1-3
17. Peter. Acts 5:15
18. David. I Chron. 21:9-14
19. Agag. I Sam. 15:33
20. Haggai and Zechariah. Ezra 5:1-2

Quiz #9

1. Nathan. II Sam. 12:7
2. Saul. Acts 8:3
3. Mary, the sister of Lazarus. John 11:2
4. Caiaphas. Matt. 26:3
5. Jeroboam. I Kings 12:26-30
6. Rehoboam. I Kings 12:1-20
7. Eve. Gen. 2:19-25

WHO? WHAT? WHERE? BIBLE QUIZ — ANSWERS

8. Paul. Acts 26:24-25
9. Elymas the sorcerer. Acts 13:4-13
10. Belshazzar. Dan. 5:1
11. Cain. Gen. 4:3
12. Jair. Judges 10:3
13. Aaron. Exodus 28:1-3
14. David. I Sam. 16:23
15. Zilpah. Gen. 30:9-13
16. Tertius. Rom. 16:22
17. Absalom. II Sam. 18:17
18. His wife. Job 2:9
19. Aaron. Lev. 10:1,2
20. God. Exodus 12:8

Quiz #10

1. Jephthah. Judges 11:34
2. Bathsheba. II Sam. 11:3
3. Matthias. Acts 1:15-26
4. Absalom. II Sam. 15:1-18
5. Timothy. I Tim. 1:2
6. Simon of Cyrene. Matt. 27:31-33
7. Nabal. I Sam. 25:11
8. Isaac. Gen. 21:1-3
9. Aaron. Ex. 4:27
10. Gabriel. Luke 1:19
11. Joab. II Sam. 11:1
12. Baal-zebub. II Kings 1:6, 16
13. Blastus. Acts 12:20
14. Salome. Matt. 14:3-11
15. The valiant men of Jabesh-gilead. I Sam. 31:12
16. Mary Magdalene. John 20:1
17. The Lord God. Gen. 3:21
18. Hilkiah. II Kings 22:8-20
19. Jehoiakim. Dan. 1:1
20. Hanani. Neh. 1:2

Quiz #11

1. Peter. Matt. 26:75
2. John the Baptist. Mark 1:6
3. Aaron. Ex. 7:1
4. Jacob. Gen. 32:24-29
5. Lot. Genesis 13:12
6. Elisha. II Kings 6:6
7. Zerubbabel. Ezra 3:8
8. Baal-berith. Judges 8:33
9. The Arabs.
10. The giant Goliath. I Sam. 17:4-11
11. Enoch. Gen. 4:17

12. Shallum. II Kings 15:10
13. Hoshea.
14. Jeroboam. I Kings 12:25
15. Abigail. I Sam. 30:5,18
16. Abimelech. Gen. 20:1-18
17. Athaliah. II Kings 8:18, 26
18. Daniel. Dan. 1:7
19. Benammi. Gen. 19:38
20. Reuben. Gen. 35:22

Quiz #12

1. John the Baptist. Mark 1:6
2. Barabbas. John 18:40
3. Jephthah. Judges 11:11
4. Abishag. I Kings 1:1-4
5. Baalpeor. Num. 25:1-9
6. Balak. Num. 22:16
7. Zeeb. Judges 7:25
8. Tubal-cain. Gen. 4:22
9. Melchizedek. Gen. 14:18
10. His two sons, Adrammelech and Sharezer. II Kings 19:37
11. The sergeants. Acts 16:35, 38
12. Shaashgaz. Esther 2:14
13. Nebuchadnezzar. Dan. 3:19-25
14. Jehoshaphat. I Kings 22:48
15. Achsah. Josh. 15:16-19
16. Phanuel. Luke 2:36-38
17. The father of Publius Acts 28:8
18. The Son of Man. Matt. 12:8
19. Jeroboam. Amos 1:1
20. Asaph. Neh. 2:8

Quiz #13

1. Caesar Augustus. Luke 2:1
2. Judas. John 12:6
3. Satan. II Cor. 4:4
4. Ibzan. Judges 12:8
5. Abner. I Sam. 14:50
6. Beh-hadad. I Kings 15:18
7. Shaphan. II Kings 22:3-7
8. His mother, Eunice. II Tim. 1:5
9. Hiram. II Sam. 5:11
10. Jason. Acts 17:5-9
11. Jesse. I Chron. 2:13, 16
12. His mother and father. I Sam. 22:3
13. Jezebel. I Kings 21:10

73

WHO? WHAT? WHERE? BIBLE QUIZ — ANSWERS

14. Those who did the will of his father in heaven. Matt. 12:50
15. Saul. I Sam. 9:2
16. Jonah. Jonah 4:6
17. Reuben. Gen. 37-22
18. Syrophoenician woman. Mark 7:28
19. The little captive maid. II Kings 5:2
20. Uriah the Hittite. II Sam. 11:15

Quiz #14

1. Haman. Esther 7:10
2. Absalom. II Sam. 13:23-29
3. Paul. Acts 14:8-15
4. Thomas. John 11:16
5. Pontius Pilate. Matt. 27:24
6. Joseph. Gen. 37:28
7. Hezekiah. Isa. 38:1-5
8. Ezekiel. Ezek. 37:1
9. Jeremiah. Jer. 38:6
10. Zacharias. Luke 1:63-64
11. Lot's wife. Gen. 19:26
12. John. Matt. 4:21
13. Herodias' daughter. Mark 6:22
14. Kish. I Sam. 9:1-2
15. Queen of Sheba. I Kings 10:2
16. Joseph called Barsabas and Matthias. Acts 1:23
17. Elon. Judges 12:11
18. Cain. Gen. 4:8
19. Abner. II Sam. 2:8
20. Ezekiel. Eze. 30:13,16

Quiz #15

1. David. Mark. 2:25
2. Jannes and Jambres. II Tim. 3:8
3. Pharaoh's daughter. Ex. 2:6
4. Jochebed. Ex. 6:20
5. Jesus. Acts 3:15
6. Potiphar. Gen. 37:36
7. Eliezer of Damascus. Gen. 15:2
8. Abdon. Judges 12:13
9. Ashpenaz. Dan. 1:3
10. Barabbas. Matt. 27:16, 26
11. Abimelech. Gen. 21:22-34
12. Benaiah. I Kings 1:38
13. Bilhah. Gen. 30:1-8
14. Carpus. II Tim. 4:13

15. Jonadad. Jer. 35:6,7
16. Samson. Judges 14:6
17. David.
18. Gamaliel. Acts 22:3
19. Gedaliah. II Kings 25:22-24
20. Elasah and Bemariah. Jer. 29:3

Quiz #16

1. Abraham. Gen. 17:5
2. Samson. Judges 15:20
3. Osnapper. Ezra 4:10
4. Zebul. Judges 9:28, 36-39
5. An unamed woman of Shunem. II Kings 4:10
6. Euodias and Syntyche. Phil. 4:2
7. Herod. Acts 23:35
8. The lost sheep of the house of Israel. Matt. 10:6
9. Geshem. Neh. 2:19; 6:1ff
10. Potiphar. Gen. 37:36
11. Tertullus. Acts. 24:5
12. John. John 19:26-27
13. Elizabeth. Luke 1:39,40
14. Lucifer. Isa. 14:12
15. Zechariah. Zech. 9:9
16. Pilate's wife. Matt. 27:19
17. Peter. Matt. 17:24-27
18. Jesus. Luke 22:31-34
19. Elisha. II Kings 4:38-41
20. Ishmael. Gen. 21:9-21

Quiz #17

1. Nicodemus. John 3:1,2
2. Esau. Gen. 25:33
3. Jezebel. I Kings 21:8-13
4. Simon the sorcerer. Acts 8:19
5. Ananias. Acts 9:17
6. The angel of the Lord. Ex. 3:2
7. Agur. Pro. 30:1
8. Nibhaz and Tartak. II Kings 17:24,31
9. Baal-hanan. I Chron. 27:28
10. James and John. Luke 9:52-56
11. Shemeber. Gen. 14:2,8,10
12. Pashhur. Jer. 21:1ff
13. His nephew. Acts 23:16-31
14. Antipas. Revelations 2:13
15. An ancient Semitic deity popular in Jerusalem and Egypt in Jere-

miah's time, when the women baked cakes used in the ritual of her worship. Jer. 7:18

16. Benaiah. II Sam. 23:22,23
17. Zipporah. Ex. 4:25
18. Melchizedek. Gen. 14:18
19. David. I Chron. 11:17-19
20. Lamech. Gen. 4:19

Quiz #18

1. Adam Gen. 2:20
2. The Pharisees John 8:15
3. Jacob Gen. 28:20-22
4. Rachel Gen. 31:34
5. Rebekah Gen. 24:20,25
6. His mother Ex. 2:7-9
7. Ahaziah II Kings 1:2
8. Baruch Jer. 36:1-8
9. Benaiah I Kings 2:25,29,46
10. Tychicus Eph. 6:21
11. Pashhur Jer. 20:1-3
12. Silas Acts 15:40 later by Timothy Acts 16:1 and Luke Acts 16:9
13. A military and political Cabal headed by Pekah II Kings 15:22-26
14. Cyrenius Luke 2:2
15. Simon of Cyrene Mark 15:21
16. Mithredath Ezra 1:8
17. Moses Deut. 32:1-48
18. Saul I Sam. 31:4
19. Hezekiah II Kings 20:7
20. The Greeks John 12:20-22

WHAT? BIBLE QUIZ — ANSWERS

WHO? WHAT? WHERE? BIBLE QUIZ — ANSWERS

Quiz #1

1. Jacob's. John 4:6
2. The ten (10) commandments.
3. Peter. John 18:15
4. The Apocalypse.
5. They returned to Jerusalem and engaged in daily worship. Acts 1:12,13
6. Pithon and Raamses. Ex. 1:11
7. He was very fat. Judges 3:17
8. Search me, O God, and know my heart. Ps. 139:23
9. To, burn his house. Judges 12:1
10. Of stealing her father's images. Gen. 31:19
11. The tribe of Levi. Ex. 6:16-20
12. She died in childbirth. I Sam. 4:20
13. Benjamin. I Sam. 9:1
14. He mourned for him and wept. II Sam. 1:12
15. Scanty and mean sacrifices and offerings to God Mal. 1
16. A blue fringed ribbon on the borders of their garments. Num. 15:38-40
17. To deliver them up to him. Josh. 2:3
18. Ai. Josh. 7:2-5
19. Almug. I Kings 10:11,12
20. Arnon. Num. 21:13

Quiz #2

1. Be born again. John 3:7
2. Shibboleth. Judges 12:6
3. The word of God. Matt. 4:4,7
4. The command of God to offer Isaac as a burnt offering. Gen. 22:2
5. Making bricks and other field service and in building treasure cities. Ex. 1:14
6. He ordered him killed by one of his soldiers. II Sam. 1:14-16
7. Because he continued to mourn for Saul whom the Lord had rejected. I Sam. 16:1
8. They rebelled against the author-
ity of Moses and Aaron. Num. 16:3
9. Reconciliation between persons or beings at variance. Rom. 5:11
10. Their staves. Num. 21:16-18
11. Half a shekel. Ex. 38:26
12. Benoni. Gen. 35:18
13. Castor and pollux. Acts 28:11
14. Cenchrea. Rom. 16:1
15. Jasper. Rev. 21:19
16. He was little of stature. Luke 19:3
17. Perverting the nation, forbidding to give tribute to Caesar, claiming himself as Christ, a king. Luke 23:1,2
18. A bullock and a ram. Num. 23:14
19. Pison, Gihon, Hiddekel, Euphrates. Gen. 2:11, 13, 14
20. The Egyptian Sea. Isa. 11:15

Quiz #3

1. Search the scriptures. John 5:39
2. Deborah. Judges 4:4
3. Solomon's temple. II Chron. 3:1
4. The Mosque of Omer, a Mohammedan place of worship.
5. She pretended to be afraid that Jacob would marry a Hittite woman. Gen. 27:46
6. The Lord's Supper.
7. It refers to the angel of death passing over the blood-sprinkled doorposts of the Children of Israel. Ex. 12:23
8. The Amalekites. I Sam. 15:3
9. To burn incense and make an atonement. Num. 16:46
10. He was refreshed and the evil spirit departed from him. I Sam. 16:23
11. They would save the lives and property of her family when they took Jericho. Josh. 2:12-14
12. Aceldama. Acts 1:19, Matt. 27:8
13. A Hebrew measure used for measuring liquids. I Kings 7:26,38
14. Death by stoning. Lev. 24:16

79

WHO? WHAT? WHERE? BIBLE QUIZ — ANSWERS

15. A net worn over the hair by Hebrew women. Isa. 3:18
16. Sapphire. Rev. 21:19
17. Philippi. Acts 16:12ff
18. Blindness. Acts 9:8-9
19. The fear of the Lord. Pro. 1:7
20. Gensis.

Quiz #4

1. Slime and pitch. Ex. 2:3
2. To ascend Mt. Nebo and die. Deut. 32:48-52
3. To bring the silver and gold into the treasury of the Lord. Josh. 6:18-19
4. Allonbacuth. Gen. 35:8
5. Bel. Isa. 46:1
6. Ungodliness. Deut. 13:13
7. An instrument for blowing the fire of a smelting furnace. Jer. 6:29
8. Belteshazzar. Dan. 1:7
9. Benjamin. Gen. 35:18
10. Bethany. John 11:1
11. Left. Eze. 39:3
12. Bul. I Kings 6:38
13. The Canaanite or Zealots which is synonymous. Matt. 104, Luke 6:15
14. The castle of the Jebusites. I Chron. 11:4-9
15. An officer in the Roman Army who commanded one hundred (100) soldiers. Acts 21:32
16. Chalcedony. Rev. 21:19
17. Sea of Tiberias. John 6:1
18. Pison. Gen. 2:11
19. Gabbatha. John 19:13
20. Being childless. I Sam. 1:10,11

Quiz #5

1. Master. John 1:38
2. A stone. John 1:42
3. Rebekah. Gen. 24:15
4. They are burned. John 15:6
5. He built an altar and offered a sacrifice. Gen. 8:20
6. To go over the Jordan. Josh. 1:2
7. Abaddon. Rev. 9:11

8. Bethesda. John 5:2
9. Emerald. Rev. 21:19
10. Zebah and Zalmunna. Judges 8:21
11. Any one-horned animal such as the rhinoceros, but the Biblical animal was two-horned. Isa. 34:7, Deut. 33:17
12. Bursts of energy I Sam. 14:36; 15:7 and fits of depression I Sam. 16:14,23
13. Sheol
14. Gihon. Gen. 2:13
15. Grasshoppers. Num. 13:33
16. Isaiah. Acts 8:30
17. Linen. I Sam. 2:18
18. The Pharisees. Acts 26:5
19. Those under his charge were carried away as prisoners. Jer. 41:10
20. The king and people repented and turned from their evil ways. Jonah 3:10

Quiz #6

1. Elijah. I Kings 17:6
2. To throw down the altar of Baal. Judges 6:25-30
3. Light was created and separated from the darkness. Gen. 1:4
4. Heaven. Gen. 1:8
5. Earth, seas, plant life. Gen. 1:10, 11
6. Sun, moon, stars. Gen. 1:14-18
7. Animal life. Gen. 1:21
8. Man. Gen. 1:27
9. Rested. Gen. 2:2
10. Jerubbaal. Judges 7:1
11. Esau was red and hairy, and Jacob was smooth. Gen. 25:25, 27:11
12. Gentleness, patience, humility and forebearance.
13. They cut off his thumbs and his great toes. Judges 1:6
14. A musical term probably refers to maiden or treble voices. I Chron. 15:20
15. Sardonyx. Rev. 21:20

WHO? WHAT? WHERE? BIBLE QUIZ — ANSWERS

16. A manifestation of God to an individual Ex. 3:2, 19:20; Gen. 18: 2:22
17. The jawbone of an ass. Judges 15:14-17
18. Luke 23:43; II Cor. 12:4; Rev. 2:7
19. Raven. Gen. 8:7
20. Rimmon. II Kings 5:18

Quiz #7

1. Had them thrown into the fiery furnace. Dan. 3:21
2. That they would be like God knowing good and evil. Gen. 3:4, 5
3. The field of blood. Acts 1:19
4. Overseer of his house. Gen. 39:4
5. To institute the passover sacrifice and feast. Ex. 12
6. Sardius. Rev. 21:20
7. Ziz. II Chron. 20:16
8. Wisdom, law, and prophecy.
9. A professed possessor of supernatural knowledge derived from the pretended ability to converse with the spirits of the dead. Isa. 8:19
10. A plant growing near Sodom which yielded cluster of bitter fruit. Deut. 32:32
11. Theudas and Judas of Galilee. Acts 5:36,37
12. Thomas. John 20:25
13. Alexander and Rufus. Mark 15: 21
14. Rings. James 2:2; Luke 15:22
15. Sheshach. Jer. 51:41
16. Hadassah. Esther 2:7
17. A coat. I Sam. 2:19
18. Milk and butter. Judges 5:25
19. Ways of pleasantness and peace. Pro. 3:17
20. Psalms.

Quiz #8

1. Babel. Gen. 11:9
2. A bullock, sheep, goat, turtle-dove, or young pigeon. Lev. 1

3. An ox goad. Judges 3:31
4. Circumcision. Ex. 4:24-25
5. The Spirit departed from Saul. I Sam. 16:14
6. Apollyon. Rev. 9:11
7. Chrysolyte. Rev. 21:20
8. Wine or other strong drink turned sour by acetous fermentation. Num. 6:3
9. Ebenezer. I Sam. 7:12
10. Miletus. Acts 20:15-17
11. Jehovah-jireh. Gen. 22:14
12. Deceitful above all things — desperately wicked. Jer. 17:9
13. Locusts and wild honey. Matt. 3: 4
14. Philippi. Acts 16:12
15. A worm. Jonah 4:7
16. Alms. Acts 3:3
17. Husks. Luke 15:16
18. The preacher. Ecc. 1:1
19. A valley of dry bones revived into living men. Eze. 37
20. The overthrow of the Edomites.

Quiz #9

1. Skins of animals. Gen. 3:21
2. Armageddon. Rev. 16:16
3. Beryl. Rev. 21:20
4. Fishermen. Matt. 4:18, Mark 1: 16
5. He ate grass as oxen, his body was wet with the dew of heaven, his hair was grown like eagle's feathers and his nails like bird's claws. Dan. 4:33
6. The gospel of Jesus Christ. Rom. 1:3
7. Gold, frankincense and myrrh. Matt. 2:11
8. Mandrakes. Gen. 30:14
9. To see the prints of the nails and to thrust his hand into Jesus' side. John 20:25
10. To speak the things that became sound doctrine and to exhort and rebuke with all authority. Titus 2:1,15

81

WHO? WHAT? WHERE? BIBLE QUIZ — ANSWERS

11. She laughed within herself. Gen. 18:12
12. The church at Rome. Rom. 1:8
13. Rock rabbits. Lev. 11:5, Prov. 30:26
14. Scapegoat. Lev. 16:20-22, Isa. 53:6
15. Nebuchadnezzar. Dan. 4:33
16. The blighting of the barren fig tree. Mark 11:12-14, 20-22
17. A bottle of water and some bread. Gen. 21:14
18. The ascription of human form, personality or attributes to God.
19. Olive. Gen. 8:11
20. Israel. Gen. 32:28

Quiz #10

1. Mankind was scattered over all the earth. Gen. 11:9
2. To take a heifer, and say that he had come to offer a sacrifice to God. I Sam. 16:2
3. Enoch. Gen. 4:17
4. They were not allowed to enter the promised land. Num. 20:12
5. Alabaster. Matt. 26:7
6. The whole armour of God. Eph. 6:11
7. Topaz. Rev. 21:20
8. Turtledove. Jer. 8:7; Song of Sol. 2:12
9. Bethel, Gilgal and Mizpeh. I Sam. 7;16
10. Returning good for evil. Rom. 12:20; Prov. 25:22
11. Jehovah-nissi. Ex. 17:15
12. Mending their nets. Matt. 4:21
13. Repent ye; for the kingdom of heaven is at hand. Matt. 3:2
14. If the Lord would deliver the children of Ammon into his hand, he would offer the first thing that came out of his house. Judges 11:30-40
15. A fleece of wool. Judges 6:36, 37
16. A fever. Mark 1:30-31
17. Valley of slaughter. Jer. 19:6
18. The announcement by Gabriel to

Mary of Nazareth that she was to bear a son, Jesus, who would have the throne of David. Luke 1:28-32
19. A coat. Gen. 37:3
20. Death. Rom. 6:23

Quiz #11

1. Pure olive oil. Ex. 27:20
2. Chrysoprasus. Rev. 21:20
3. Sycamore. Luke 19:4
4. Two (2) turtles of two (2) young pigeons Lev. 12:8; Num. 6:10
5. Eternal life. Rom. 6:23
6. Women: woman of Timmah, a Gaza harlot, Delilah of Sorek. Judges 15:1; 16:1, 4-20
7. The chief judicial council or supreme court of the Jews.
8. Jabesh-gilead. I Sam. 11:1-7
9. Venison. Gen. 27:3,4
10. The Sanhedrin.
11. Bozez and Seneh. I Sam. 14:4
12. Shadrack. Dan. 1:7
13. Shear-jashub. Isa. 7:3
14. A divine communication Rom. 3:2, Heb. 5:12 or the person through which the message was received. Acts 7:38
15. Peter. Acts 1:13
16. Hymenaeus and Philetus. II Tim. 2:17,18
17. Old cast clouts and old rotten rags. Jer. 38:11
18. Canaan. Ex. 3:8
19. An unbeliever or disbeliever especially one who disbelieves in Christianity. II Cor. 6:15, I Tim. 5:8
20. Sitting at the receipt of custom. Matt. 9:9

Quiz #12

1. Jacinth. Rev. 21:20
2. That he would receive the earrings of the prey of each man. Judges 8:24
3. Zaphenathpaneah. Gen. 41:45

WHO? WHAT? WHERE? BIBLE QUIZ — ANSWERS

4. They cut off his head and circulated it among the villages of the Philistines, put his armour in the house of Ashtaroth and fastened his body to the wall of Beth-shan. I Sam. 31:8-11
5. Oxen. I Kings 19:19
6. Ass and ox. Deut. 22:10
7. Zech. 2:12.
8. Jericho. Deut. 34:3
9. The Pentateuch.
10. Philip, Andrew and Peter. John 1:44
11. Quail. Ex. 16:3,8,13
12. Shebah. Gen. 26:32, 33
13. Earrings. Ex. 32:3
14. Abstain from pollutions of idols, from fornication, from things strangled, and from blood. Acts 15:20,29
15. Gilboa. II Sam. 1:21
16. Greek speaking Jews of the dispersion who had adopted Greek habits and customs. Acts 6:1; 9:29
17. A heart attack. I Sam. 25:37
18. A great earthquake. Acts 16:25. 26
19. The glorification of faithful married love, the betrothed lovers being regarded as already husband and wife.
20. Isaiah.

Quiz #13

1. Amethyst. Rev. 21:20
2. Zedekiah. II Kings 24:17
3. That the worship of the true God would continue among his descendants. Gen. 9:21-27
4. A ritualistic offering presented to God, usually of a non-living object in contrast with animal sacrifices. Lev. 2:4,12
5. Shibboleth. Judges 12:4-6
6. A golden earring and bracelets. Gen. 24:22
7. Seir. Gen. 32:3; Num. 24:18; Judges 5:4

8. Greek.
9. Hebrew.
10. Handkerchiefs and aprons. Acts 19:12
11. The charge was made against the individual for the responsibility of life or death. Josh. 2:19; I Kings 2.37
12. An understanding heart. I Kings 3:9
13. Kirjath-arba. Gen. 23:2
14. Jupiter. Acts 14:12
15. Hexateuch.
16. It is to be hewn down and cast into the fire. Matt. 7:19
17. Hyssop. Ex. 12:22
18. A mother of nations. Gen. 17:16
19. From Abraham down to the death of Christ. Acts 7:1-53
20. Keeping the flock of Jethro. Ex. 3:2

Quiz #14

1. Pearls. Rev. 21:21
2. Pure gold. Rev. 21:21
3. Ox. Deut. 25:4
4. Palm trees. Ps. 92:12
5. Hephzibah. Isa. 62:4
6. Mercurius. Acts 14:12
7. Hezekiah. II Kings 18:4
8. Tabitha. Acts 9:36
9. Jordan. Gen. 13:10,11
10. The Fifthieth (50). Lev. 25:10
11. The King's Highway. Num. 20:17, 21:22
12. A blemish, blindness, lameness, a flat nose, anything superfluous, a brokenfoot, a brokenhand, crookback, dwarfness, scurvy or scabbed. Lev. 21:18-20
13. The snuffing out of life. Prov. 13:9-20:20
14. The mirrors of women ministering at the door of the tabernacle of the congregation. Ex. 38:8
15. They did the service of the tabernacle of the congregation. Num. 18:6

WHO? WHAT? WHERE? BIBLE QUIZ — ANSWERS

16. Thunder and lightning. Ex. 19:6-20:18
17. Phillipi and Thessalonica.
18. Maher-shalal-hash-boz. Isa. 8:1-4
19. Mara. Ruth 1:20
20. Blasphemy against the Holy Ghost. Matt. 12:31

Quiz #15

1. That he would be saved when Jerusalem was captured. Jer. 38:7-13
2. The substance of things hoped for, the evidence of things not seen. Heb. 11:1
3. Righteousness. Prov. 14:34
4. Their sin was very grievous. Gen. 18:20
5. They and their families were thrown into the lion's den. Dan. 6:24
6. Meat. I Cor. 8:13
7. Cruelty, oppression and idolatry.
8. Shallum. II Kings 15:13
9. Sardis. Rev. 3:1-6
10. Laodicea. Rev. 3:14-22
11. Unto them were committed the oracles of God. Rom. 3:1,2
12. The cross and related truths to the death of Christ. I Cor. 2:2
13. Locust and wild honey. Matt. 3:4
14. To walk in God's ways and to keep His commandments. I Kings 2:1-3
15. All the garments which Dorcas had made while she was alive. Acts 9:39
16. His donkey. Num. 22:33
17. Athens-mentioned in Acts.
18. Have mercy on us, O, Lord, Thou son of David. Matt. 20:30-31
19. Judaizing teachers. Gal. 2:15-18
20. A hailstorm. Josh. 10:8-11

Quiz #16

1. Calebephrathah. I Chron. 2:24
2. Calno. Isaiah 10:9
3. Tender meat of kids. Gen. 27:9, 14,17
4. A staff borne by a ruler to indicate his authority. Esther 4:11, Gen. 49:10
5. A Division inside a religious group or sect formed by a difference of opinion. I Cor. 12:25
6. Meshach. Dan. 1:7
7. Jordan. Judges 3:28
8. Thyatira. Rev. 2:20-24
9. A stumbling block. I Cor. 1:23
10. A throne and one that sat on it. Rev. 4:2
11. She would give him unto the Lord all the days of his life. I Sam. 1:11
12. Christian morality rather than doctrines. James 1:22-2:20
13. Greek. Gal. 2:3
14. James, I & II Peter, I, II & III John, Jude.
15. Hiram, king of Tyre. II Sam. 5:11
16. They sang a song of rejoicing. Ex. 15:1
17. Circumcision. Josh. 5:2,3
18. Ass. Matt. 21:1-11
19. Bethsaida, Capernaum, Chorazin. Matt. 11:21-23
20. Beulah. Isa. 62:4

Quiz #17

1. To come and have the honor of completing the conquest of Rabbah himself. II Sam. 12:27-28
2. Bezar, Ramoth, Golan. Deut. 4:41-43
3. Greek, Latin, Hebrew. Luke 23:38
4. Boanerges-Sons of Thunder. Mark 3:17
5. Weaving and dyeing. Isa. 63:1-3; Gen. 36:33
6. Capernaum. Matt. 9:1
7. Chemosh. Num. 21:29
8. Gezer. I Kings 9:16
9. An offering dedicated to God and therefore not free for other purposes. Mark 7:11-13
10. Cos. Acts 21:1

WHO? WHAT? WHERE? BIBLE QUIZ — ANSWERS

11. The butler charged with testing wines served to his royal master. Gen. 40:11; I Kings 10:5
12. A roll authorizing his work. Ezra 6:1-5
13. Silversmith. Acts 19:24
14. A figure of speech for paradise. Luke 16:22
15. A bow. Gen. 9:13
16. A pit. Gen. 37:22
17. They were compelled to make bricks, but no straw had been given them. Ex. 5:15
18. Olive oil. Ex. 27:20
19. The Amalekites.
20. A godly sorrow for sin, accompanied with a change of purpose and of life.

Quiz #18
1. Cana John 21:2
2. Valley of Zeboim I Sam. 13:18
3. Secretaries, recorders and clerks to kings, governments and the temple organization. II Kings 12:10
4. Abed-nego Dan. 1:7
5. Iran
6. A short, thick instrument for grinding and pounding grains, spices, etc. in a mortar. Prov. 27:22
7. They conspired in the trial of Jesus. They were enemies before, but by a common hatred of Jesus, they became friends. Luke 23:12
8. "My God, My God, why hast thou forsaken me?" Matt. 27:46
9. She conceived and bore a child when she was old. II Kings 4:17
10. Euroclydon Acts 27:14
11. Put them out of the land. I Sam. 28:3
12. An apron-like garment worn under the breastplate of the high priest. Ex. 28:6-14
13. Gopher Gen. 6:14
14. Matthew, Mark, Luke and John
15. The unbelief of the people in Him Ex. 4:1 and his lack of eloquence Ex. 4:10
16. Their throat is an open sepulchre. Rom. 3:13
17. Foolishness I Cor. 1:23
18. A man who is a householder Matt. 20:1
19. Seth Gen. 4:25
20. Put him in prison Gen. 39:20

WHERE? BIBLE QUIZ — ANSWERS

WHO? WHAT? WHERE? BIBLE QUIZ — ANSWERS

Quiz #1

1. Tarsus. Acts 11:25
2. In John's home. John 19:27
3. Cana of Galilee. John 2:1
4. On Mars hill in Athens. Acts 17: 22-23
5. On the Isle of Patmos. Rev. 1:9
6. At the right hand of God. Heb. 12:2
7. In Mt. Ephraim between Ramah and Bethel. Judges 4:5
8. In the cave of Machpelah. Gen. 23:19
9. On Mt. Moriah. II Chron. 3:1
10. Mizpeh. I Sam. 10:17
11. Bethlehem. I Sam. 16:1
12. Adramythium. Acts 27:2
13. At Kadesh, in the desert of Zin. Num. 20:1
14. Lydda. Acts 9:32-35
15. Bethel and Dan. I Kings 12:29
16. Aijalon. Judges 12:12
17. Arvad. Ezek. 27:8,11
18. Land of Shinar. Gen. 11:2,9
19. In the Nile. Ex. 2:5
20. Beer. Num. 21:16-18

Quiz #2

1. Bethabara. John 1:28
2. Bethlehem. Matt. 2:1
3. Shamir in Mt. Ephraim. Judges 10:1
4. In the land of Goshen. Gen. 46: 29
5. In the temple as he ministered in the priest's office. Luke 1:11
6. Jerusalem. II Sam. 11:1
7. Shushan. Esther 1:2
8. Valley of Achor. Josh. 7:24-26
9. Under an oak tree called Allon-bacuth near Bethel. Gen. 35:8
10. Appii-Forum. Acts 28:15
11. Baal-hamon. Song of Solomon 8: 11
12. Well of Beer-lahai-roi. Gen. 16:7, 14
13. Beer-sheba. Gen. 21:22-34
14. Ephrath. Gen. 35:16-19
15. Jerusalem. John 5:2

16. In the blood. Lev. 17:11
17. Bochim. Judges 2:1-5
18. Zelah in the sepulchre of Kish. II Sam. 21:14
19. In the palace at Shushan by the Ulai river. Dan. 8:2
20. Bethlehem. Gen. 35:16-19

Quiz #3

1. Egypt. Matt. 2:14
2. Ur. Gen. 11:31
3. Jerusalem. Luke 2:42
4. Bethlehem. Judges 12:8,10
5. At Shechem. Josh. 24:1
6. Bethlehem. Ruth 1:19; 4:9-11
7. Cenchrea. Rom. 16:1
8. Jericho. Luke 19:1
9. Zelzah. I Sam. 10:2
10. In the school of Tyrannus. Acts 19:9
11. Under an oak tree near Shechem. Gen. 35:4
12. On. Gen. 41:45
13. Pandan-Aram. Gen. 28:2,6
14. Bethsaida. John 1:44
15. Cave at Makkedah. Joshua 10:16
16. Mt. Pisgah. Num. 23:14
17. Shiloh. I Sam 3
18. Edrei. Num. 21:33-35
19. Bethany in the home of Simon the leper. Matt. 26:6 ff
20. On the island of Melita. Acts 28: 1-6

Quiz #4

1. In the temple at Jerusalem. John 10:23
2. Bethany. John 11:1
3. Antioch. Acts 11:19-26
4. Bathpeor. Deut. 34:6
5. Caesarea. Acts 10:1
6. Jerusalem. Matt. 21:1 John 12:12-13
7. Antioch of Pisidia. Acts 13:14-46-47
8. Taberan. Num. 11:1-3
9. Zorah. Judges 13:1-5
10. Jerusalem. Matt. 2:1
11. Tob. Judges 11:3,5

WHO? WHAT? WHERE? BIBLE QUIZ — ANSWERS

12. Shechem. Josh. 24:32
13. Topheth. Jer. 7:31 II Kings 23:10
14. Thyatira. Acts 16:14
15. Babel. Gen. 11:9
16. Capernaum. Mark 2:1-5
17. Isle of Patmos. Rev. 1:9
18. Home of Philip in Caesarea. Acts 21:8-11
19. Gilgal. I Sam. 11:15
20. Gob. II Sam. 21:19

Quiz #5
1. Nazareth. Luke 2:39
2. Outside the town of Bethany. John 11:30
3. At the well of Haran. Gen. 29:1-14
4. Kadeshnaphtali. Judges 4:6
5. From abroad. Judges 12:9
6. To Midian. Ex. 2:15
7. Antioch. Acts 13:1-4
8. On the mountains of Araret. Gen. 8:4
9. Baal-shalisha. II Kings 4:42-44
10. Ezion-geber. I Kings 22:48
11. Perga in Pamphylia. Acts 13:13
12. Ekron. II Kings 1:2
13. Mizpah. II Kings 25:25
14. Kibroth-hattaavah. Num. 11:34
15. Lo-debar. II Sam. 9:4 ff
16. By the river of Chebar. Ezek. 1:1
17. In the land of Uz. Job 1:1
18. Tarshesh. Jonah 1:3
19. On the road to Emmaus. Luke 24:13-15
20. On a mountain. Matt. 3:13-19

Quiz #6
1. Bethlehem. Luke 2:3,4
2. In the Garden of Eden. Gen. 2:8
3. Egypt. Ex. 12:29
4. Paphos. Acts 13:6,7
5. Moab. Ruth 1:1
6. Lystra. Acts 14:8,11
7. Egypt. Ex. 1
8. At Jacob's well near Sychar. John 4:6
9. In a well. II Sam. 17:18-20

10. Near Bethany. Luke 24:50,51
11. Tyre in Syria. Acts 21:1-4
12. Babylon. Ezra 7:6-9
13. In the house of Mary, Mother of John Mark. Acts 12:12 1
14. In the synagogue. Acts 17:1,2
15. On the island of Melita. Acts 28:3
16. In the plains of Mamre. Gen. 18:1
17. In the midst of a valley of dry bones. Ezek. 37:1
18. Calvary. Luke 23:33
19. By the river Ulai. Dan. 8:2
20. Mt. Hor. Num. 20:27-29

Quiz #7
1. Haran. Gen. 11:32
2. In the Jordan river. Mark 1:9
3. Hazer in Canaan. Judges 4:2
4. Shechem. Judges 8:31
5. Zarephath. I Kings 17:21
6. Tarsus. Acts 9:11
7. In the garden of Gethsemane. Matt. 26:47 ff
8. Gibeah. I Sam. 10:26
9. In the house of Aquila and Priscilla. Acts 18:26
10. In the pool of Siloam. John 9:6,7
11. At the Jordan river. II Kings 2:1-11
12. Sichem in the plain of Moab. Gen. 12:6
13. Jerusalem. Matt. 23:37
14. In heaven. Matt. 6:20,21
15. Damascus. Gal. 1:17
16. In the camel's furniture. Gen. 31:34
17. On the roof of her house. Josh. 2:6
18. Shiloh near Sichem. Josh. 18:1
19. By the river Ahava. Ezra 8:15, 21, 31
20. Beth-shan. I Sam. 31:10

Quiz #8
1. Cassarea and Tarsus. Acts 9:30
2. Egypt. Gen. 12:10
3. Pirathon. Judges 12:15

WHO? WHAT? WHERE? BIBLE QUIZ — ANSWERS

4. By the brook Cherith. I Kings 17:5
5. Gerar. Gen. 20:1-3
6. Ophir. I Kings 10:11
7. Gibeon. II Sam. 21:9
8. In caves and dens. Judges 6:2
9. Nob. I Sam. 21:1-6
10. In prison. Matt. 14:1-12
11. Anathoth in the land of Benjamin. Jer. 1:1
12. Arabia. Gal. 1:17
13. Into Geshur. II Sam. 13:38
14. Capernaum. Mark 1:30-31
15. Salem, afterward named Jerusalem. Gen. 13:18
16. Bethphage. Matt. 21:1
17. Fair Haven near Lasea. Acts 27:8
18. Aphek. I Sam. 4:1 ff
20. The plains of Mamre. Gen. 18:1

Quiz #9

1. The home of Mary, John's mother. Acts 12:12
2. Mesapotamia. Acts 7:2
3. Camon. Judges 10:5
4. Antioch. Gal. 2:11
5. Bethsaida. John 9:10
6. In his palace in Samaria. II Kings 15:22-26
7. Iconium. Acts 13:51
8. Jericho. Josh. 2:1-24
9. In the court of Pharaoh.
10. The bottomless pit. Rev. 9:11
11. To the mountains to dwell in a cave. Gen. 19:30
12. Adullam. I Sam. 22:1
13. Anathoth. Jer. 1:1
14. Derbe or Lystra. Acts 16:1
15. The threshing floor of Atad. Gen. 50:10
16. Shechem. I Kings 12:1
17. Zoar. Gen. 19:22
18. To visit Elizabeth in the hill country. Luke 1:39-40
19. Shechem in Mt. Ephriam. I Kings 12:25
20. In the city of David (Jerusalem). I Kings 22:50

Quiz #10

1. Jerusalem. Acts 9:26
2. The land of Tob. Judges 11:5
3. At Ziklag. II Sam. 1:1
4. At Ramah. I Sam. 7:17
5. Ophrah. Judges 6-8
6. Under a fig tree. John 1:48
7. Under an oak tree in Ophrah. Judges 6:11
8. In the carcass of a lion. Judges 14:8
9. At the gate of the temple which is called Beautiful. Acts 3:3
10. Mt. Ephraim. Judges 17:1
11. Berea. Acts 17:10
12. At the bedside of his dying mother. Gen. 35:18
13. Into Galilee. Matt. 4:12
14. Cyprus. Acts. 15:39
15. At the river of Ahava. Ezra 8:21
16. Mt. Ephraim. Josh. 24:30
17. Carmel. I Sam. 25:2,3
18. Dalmanutha. Mark 8:10
19. Mt. Hor. Num 20:22-28
20. Beth-shan. I Sam. 31:10

Quiz #11

1. Caesarea. Acts 25:1-4
2. Caesarea Philippi. Matt. 16:13
3. Tyre. Acts 21:5
4. Shiloh.
5. In Mt. Gilboa. I Sam. 31:8
6. Valley of Shaveh. Gen. 14:17
7. Mt. Carmel. I Kings 18:17-46
8. Paran. Gen. 21:21
9. Penuel. Gen. 32:30
10. Pergamos. Acts 2:13
11. Colossae.
12. Babylon. II Chron. 33:11
13. Inside pitchers. Judges 7:16ff
14. Shiloh. Josh. 18:1ff
15. Mt. Ebal. Josh. 8:30-35
16. Elah. I Sam. 17:2, 19ff
17. Joppa. Acts 9:36
18. Kir. II Kings 16:9
19. Babylon. II Kings 25:8
20. Geshur. II Sam. 13:37

WHO? WHAT? WHERE? BIBLE QUIZ — ANSWERS

Quiz #12

1. By a fountain near Shur. Gen. 16:7
2. Zorah. Judges 13:2
3. Ephesus. Acts 19:27
4. In the sand. Ex. 2:12
5. Tarshish. Jonah 1:3
6. Land of Judah. Ruth 1:7
7. Anathoth. I Kings 1:7
8. Mt. Sinai. Ex. 24:18ff
9. From the sacred altar which God kindled when the tabernacle was consecrated and was to be kept burning continually. Lev. 1:13
10. Armageddon. Rev. 16:16
11. In Philippi by a river. Acts 16:12-14
12. Jericho. Mark 10:46
13. Aphek. I Kings 20:30
14. Bethel. Gen. 12:8
15. Lehi. Judges 15:1-20
16. In the house of Ashtaroth. I Sam. 31:10
17. Carmel. I Sam. 15:12
18. Ur. Gen. 11:28
19. In His own country. Mark 1:1-6
20. Mt. Ephraim. Josh. 24:33

Quiz #13

1. Gilgal. II Kings 4:38
2. Wilderness of Judah, south of Arad. Judges 1:16
3. In the home of Nisroch, his god in Nineveh. II Kings 19:36,37
4. Babylon, Cuthah, Ava, Hamath, and Sepharvaim. II Kings 17:24
5. In the Lord and the power of His might. Eph. 6:10
6. Valley of Ajalon. Josh. 10:12
7. Egypt. Gen. 21:21
8. Antioch. Acts 11:28;21:10
9. In the wilderness of Judaea. Matt. 3:1
10. In the Jordan river. Matt. 3:6
11. Moab. Ruth 1:4
12. Cana of Galilee. John 21:2
13. Ararat. II kings 19:37
14. Athens. Acts 17:19

15. Pontus. Acts 18:2
16. Ashdod. I Sam. 5
17. Athens. Acts 17:22
18. Bathing on the roof top. II Sam. 11:2,3
19. Jericho. II Sam. 10:5
20. Damascus. I Kings 15:18

Quiz #14

1. At the palace of Caiaphas. Matt. 26:3-5
2. On Mt. Carmel. I Kings 18:44
3. Seleucia. Acts 13:4
4. Mt. of Olives. John 7:53; 8:1
5. Shiloh. Judges 21:15-24
6. Between Mizpeh and Shen. I Sam. 7:12
7. Elim. Ex. 15:27
8. In the presence of God. Luke 1:19
9. Gadara. Mark 5:1-20
10. Mt. Horeb. Ex. 33:6
11. Lystra. Acts 14:6,19
12. Sychar, Samaria. John 4:5
13. Caesarea Philippi. Matt. 16:13-16
14. Nineveh. Jonah 1:2
15. Sodom. Gen. 14:12
16. On the sea. Matt. 14:22-26
17. To Galilee. Luke 4:14
18. Jerusalem. John 21:23ff
19. Above the mercy seat, between the cheribims. Ex. 25:22
20. Babylon. Dan. 7:1

Quiz #15

1. From India to Ethiopia over one hundred twenty-seven (127) provinces. Esther 1:1
2. Destruction.
3. At the brook Kidron. II Chron. 15:16
4. In a house in Damascus. Acts 9:10-11
5. Rome.
6. Garden of Gethsemane. John 18:10-11
7. The plain of Dura. Dan. 3:1
8. Mt. Ebal. Josh. 8:33
9. Into the wilderness. Matt. 4:1, Mark 1:12, Luke 4:1

WHO? WHAT? WHERE? BIBLE QUIZ — ANSWERS

10. Fifteen (15) furlongs from Jerusalem. John 11:18
11. Top of a hill by Hebron. Judges 16:3
12. Three (3) on the east of the Jordan river and three (3) on the west. Deut. 4:41-43
13. Askelon where he slew thirty (30) men. Judges 14:19
14. Shechem. Judges 9:1ff
15. Timnath. Judges 14:5,6
16. Bethlehem-judah. Ruth 1:1,2
17. In the plain of Jordan or Zarthan. I Kings 7:46
18. To Zarephath. I Kings 17:9
19. Jezreel. II Kings 9:15
20. Jerusalem but not in the sepulchres of the kings. II Chron. 28:27

Quiz #16

1. Tekoa. Amos 1:1
2. Rephidim. Ex. 17:8-16
3. Gadara. Matt. 8:28-34
4. Ezion-geber. I Kings 9:26
5. Moriah. Gen. 22:2
6. Life.
7. In a tomb of Joseph of Arimathaea near where he was crucified. John 19:41
8. The land of the Philistines. II Kings 8:2
9. To Babylon. II Kings 24:15
10. A mountain in Israel. Eze. 40:2
11. Jerusalem-pool of Bethesda. John 5:19
12. Nazareth. Matt. 2:23
13. By a fountain in Jezreel. I Sam. 29:1
14. The east border of Jericho. Josh. 4:19
15. Lachish. II Kings 18:14,17
16. Megiddo. II Kings 9:27
17. Zair. II Kings 8:21
18. Eschol. Num. 13:23
19. Hebron. II Sam. 15:9
20. Hebron. II Sam. 3:27

Quiz #17

1. In the home of O bed-edom near Jerusalem. II Sam. 6:1-12
2. Mt. of Olives. Matt. 24-25
3. Paran. Num. 13:1-3
4. Riblah. II Kings 23:33ff
5. Endor. I Sam. 28:7-25
6. Bethel. II Kings 2:23
7. Lydda. Acts 9:38
8. The land of Nod. Gen. 4:16
9. Kedesh-naphtali. Judges 4:6
10. Jezreel. I Kings 21:1
11. Nahanaim. II Sam. 2:8
12. Mesopotamia Gen. 24:10
13. Garden of Gethsemane. Mark 14:31-45
14. Gaza. Judges 16:1
15. Wilderness of Sin. Ex. 16:1-22
16. Wilderness of Paran. Num. 10:11, 12
17. Pool of Samaria. I Kings 22:38
18. Jericho. Josh. 5:13
19. Gibeon. II Sam. 20:8-12
20. Gibeon. Josh. 10:10-15

Quiz #18

1. Lake of Gennesaret Luke 5:1-3
2. Mt. Horeb Ps. 106:19ff
3. Egypt I kings 11:40
4. In hell Luke 16:24
5. Judaea John 3:22
6. In his home on his knees praying Dan. 6:10-17
7. Beer-sheba I kings 19:3
8. Aphek I Sam. 29:1
9. Samaria II Kings 10:1
10. Riblah II kings 25:7
11. Mahanaim II Sam. 17:27
12. Taanaeh Judges 5:19
13. The home of Eli in Shiloh I Sam. 1:24
14. In the temple Luke 2:46
15. Kirjath-jearim Jer. 26:20
16. Dothan II Kings 6:13, 18
17. The valley of Salt II Kings 14:7
18. Near Damascus Acts 9:3
19. Jerusalem Luke 2:22
20. Jerusalem John 2:13,15